Youth policy in Armenia

An international perspective

Jan Sipos
Milosz Czerniejewski
Peter Lauritzen
Joanne Hunting
Gavan Titley
Ditta Dolejsiova
Howard Williamson

Council of Europe Publishing

Cover design and layout: Documents and Publishing Production Department (SPDP), Council of Europe

Council of Europe Publishing
F-67075 Strasbourg Cedex
http://book.coe.int

ISBN 978-92-871-6627-2
© Council of Europe, October 2009
Printed at the Council of Europe

The international reviews of national youth policy conducted by the Council of Europe inevitably address and comment rather more on matters of concern and contention. These are sometimes identified by the nations under review as priority areas for focus, and sometimes by the international review team during its reflections and deliberations.

The raising of such issues is intended to contribute to debate rather than dispute – to encourage a constructive interrogation of the relevant territory rather than destructive dismissal of the critique.

The international review team hopes that this will be the case for this report as much as it was for those that preceded it.

Contents

Executive summary

The 13th Council of Europe international review of national youth policy is the first to be conducted in a Commonwealth of Independent States country that was formerly a member of the Soviet Union. Armenia is distinct for other, more traditional reasons – not least its historical claim to being the first Christian country. Today, well over 90% of its population are ethnic Armenians with a declared membership of the Armenian Apostolic Church.

Armenia has had a troubled and often traumatic history and still faces significant social, political and economic challenges. Making sense of youth policy and understanding the circumstances of young people is not possible without reference to the delicate and difficult circumstances faced by the country, which in the past have led to significant waves of political and economic migration.

Armenia's independent constitution was first adopted in 1995 and Armenia became a member of the Council of Europe in 2001. The international review's reference to "perspective" is intentional, for youth policy – like the country itself – is young and still rapidly developing. This perspective seeks to engage with youth policy in Armenia from a position of "critical complicity": it hopes that the observations made, even those that provoke the most intense criticism, will support the constructive development of Armenia's youth policy.

Youth policy in Armenia is formally defined as "serving the needs of young people aged between 16 and 30". Youth policy itself is officially concerned with creating the conditions (socio-economic, legal, politic-al, spiritual, cultural and organisational) under which young people may realise their potential and thereby benefit their society. There are, however, competing definitions of "youth policy" in different documents, with different aspirations attached to each. Nevertheless, there has been a gradual refinement of the principles and framework of youth policy over time, as Armenia moves towards the establishment of a youth law. And, despite the huge pressure on public resources in a country confronted by significant levels of poverty, there has been a dramatic growth in financial commitment in support of youth programmes. Furthermore, a dedicated youth minister with deputy minister status within the Ministry of Sport and Youth Affairs has been making transparent efforts to strengthen the structures for the delivery of youth policy. There is, as a result, considerable activity at the centre of governance and in the capital city of Yerevan, although youth policy development at regional and local level remains in a relatively embryonic form. The nature of co-ordination between ministries, between government and international non-governmental organisations (NGOs) (of which there are a substantial number in Armenia), across the national youth NGOs of Armenia and within the *marzes* (the local authorities) has also been a cause for concern. Youth participation in decision-making processes was considered to be very variable. Despite some youth councils with high-level contacts, the National Youth Council was perceived as a closed "club".

In relation to the domains of youth policy, a range of challenges was identified. Armenia is going through the complex process of modernising its systems of education, training and the labour market and thus much remains uncertain and in flux. Nevertheless, in formal education, it will need to consider the balance between university and vocational learning, particularly in the context of the credibility of the qualifications awarded by many of its private, non-accredited universities. There may be a need for greater attention to teaching and learning styles, a stronger emphasis on information and guidance systems and a serious appraisal of the role and function of "non-formal" education in the learning pathways of young people. Within the labour market, the current focus on enterprise support is worthy of further development.

The young people of Armenia face a range of health issues (not least concerning physical fitness and sexual health) for which there do not appear to be robust policy responses, though there are some pilot initiatives. A particular focus needs to be placed on the question of young people's awareness of, as well as access to, health services. In housing, there is an intense shortage of available accommodation for young people, especially in Yerevan. Young people generally "get by", but there is a strong case for the development of a youth housing strategy which takes a range of different models of provision into account.

In certain areas of youth policy, such as social protection and family policy, the international review team felt it did not secure sufficient understanding to advance a perspective. With regard to leisure, however, the team was impressed by the mixture of traditional cultural pursuits with more contemporary leisure interests, though there was a serious question about the extent to which young people had access to the latter.

A more calibrated and individualised approach to youth justice would appear to merit consideration, given the current somewhat basic approach – though clearly this has potentially demanding resource implications. In relation to military service, the Armenian army is the largest youth organisation in the country and is greatly respected by young people. Any alternatives to military service are only a recent development for young men, and they are considered by external international commentators to be exceptionally punitive. Concern has also been expressed about the ill-treatment of conscripts: consideration might be given to improving the conditions of young men in the army, including training for future occupations. Nevertheless, the overwhelming trust in the army is one component of the traditional values and belief structure of young Armenians, which also includes their continuing attachment to the Armenian Apostolic Church (though there are concerns that this may now be starting to dissipate).

Despite considerable public rhetoric about youth participation, there remains a significant lack of trust in formal institutions (arguably a legacy of communism), which has impeded the promotion of youth involvement. Moreover, it appears that certain opportunities do not even appear to be extended to some sub-sections of the youth population. On other "cross-cutting" issues, there are huge challenges related to social inclusion, which cannot simply be left to "the market", as some people suggest. Youth information services are underdeveloped and would benefit from exploring models from other countries, especially as access to new technologies improves and the expansion of regional youth centres takes hold.

Young people in Armenia stand to gain a great deal from engagement with the European Union's youth programmes and from participation in youth activities run by the Council of Europe. This may help to open up Armenia's intellectual and conceptual, if not (yet) its political and geographical borders. It will certainly encourage a positive experience of mobility and internationalism, which is currently often not the case for some young Armenians who are subject to trafficking or form part of the international labour force of migrant workers.

On matters that contribute to supporting youth policy, youth research in Armenia did not appear to play much part in influencing the direction of youth policy. Indeed, it was not clear how much youth research was going on. Nor was it clear how much training, if any, is available for individuals working with young people (though a lot was learned about the thousands of lawyers and nurses training in Armenia each year). Finally, it was unclear how good practice was disseminated and what kinds of platform for dialogue existed. All three issues require attention if youth policy in Armenia is to move forward in an informed and confident manner.

Even though Armenia has recently endorsed a State Youth Policy Strategy, the debate on youth policy is, in many ways, just beginning. It is a debate that must be taken beyond the "inner circle" that has, to its credit, driven youth policy and practice so far. It is also a debate that must find a path between tradition and modernity, reflecting the cultures of young people and the values of Armenian society. Finally, it is a debate that has to tread between an "affirmative" position characteristic of traditional Armenia and an "anticipatory" position that looks to the future of Armenia.

Preface

Yerevan, the capital city of Armenia, could (almost) be anywhere in Europe: a bustling metropolis of wide roads, new vehicles, leisure choices and a variety of restaurants. It seems almost familiar, but not quite, because there are also numerous residual signs of its communist (Soviet) inheritance: fewer fast-food outlets than one might expect and less evidence of the incessant development and re-development of commercial and consumer activity than would typically be found elsewhere. Nevertheless, it conveys an atmosphere of relative affluence and relaxed consumption.

Yet, minutes from the city centre, one sees a very different picture – former Soviet tower blocks and cramped living apartments with drying washing hanging on virtually every balcony. Roads are full of potholes, over which older, rustier vehicles negotiate their route, and people in drab and worn clothing shop in traditional markets and at small kiosks selling confectionery and cigarettes. Not much further afield, children and young people grow up in housing with corrugated iron roofs and no direct running water – although, increasingly, they may be living relatively close to new, gated suburban communities constructed to standards expected in better-off parts of the United States.

Armenia is, then, simply from superficial and immediate observation, a land of contradictions and these contradictions become more frequent and more pronounced the more one explores and probes beneath the surface. There is not just one, but many crossroads where choices have to be made. One of those choices concerns the structure, scope and substance of Armenia's policies for its 800 000 or so young people.

Chapter 1: introduction

This is the 13th international review of national youth policy to be carried out by the Directorate of Youth and Sport of the Council of Europe. The first took place in Finland in 1997 and, since then, there have been various revisions to the process, which are discussed below, since each review in one way or another explored uncharted waters. The review of Armenia, however, was especially challenging, as it was the first CIS[1] country to seek such a youth policy review and, as such, had far fewer reference points than any other country hitherto reviewed. The countries previously reviewed[2] often had some "connecting strands" in their particular approaches to the formulation and execution of youth policy, or at least a common attachment to the European Union, either through established or new membership (for example, the Netherlands or Cyprus), an established relationship (for example, Norway), candidacy (for example, Lithuania) or reasonable prospects of joining (for example, Romania). As such, there were processes linking them to the European Commission White Paper on Youth (European Commission 2001), which is quite irrelevant to Armenia in formal terms, though it may be of strategic interest. Thus, most members of the international review team were starting from a "blank sheet of paper", with their reference points largely being countries of a comparable size (such as Wales, Latvia or Slovenia). Three members of the review team, however, were from Poland and Slovakia and therefore able to communicate in Russian, as well as having some shared cultural traditions and experiences of a communist past.

Without a national report[3] to serve as a foundation stone for the international team's enquiry, questions posed were always tentative and sometimes naïve and, though the team members learned much during their two visits, they left Armenia with many questions still unanswered and awaiting documentation they had requested. Missing information included:

---

1. Commonwealth of Independent States – formed by a number of countries from the now disbanded Soviet Union.
2. Finland, the Netherlands, Sweden, Romania, Spain, Estonia, Luxembourg, Lithuania, Malta, Norway, Cyprus and Slovakia.
3. The *Armenian Youth National Report* was received by the international team towards the end of May 2006. It is this edition that is referred to throughout this publication. It is an impressively thorough document, using both existing data and material from a specially commissioned survey of 1 000 young people (0.012% of the youth population). Different sections strike rather different balances between empirical description of the current social condition of youth in Armenia, analysis of issues and advocacy for measures that should be implemented in the future. The similar title mentioned in the bibliography below is an edited version (2008) of the report received by the international team and cannot be used for accurate reference to quotations made hereafter.

- figures concerning military service: those involved, those doing alternative service and those avoiding service altogether;

- an abstract of the Youth Law that was imminent by the time of the second visit;

- details of former Komsomol and Pioneer[4] property: extent, location, current use, responsibility;

- information about administrative regulations and procedures for the registration of non-governmental organisations (NGOs);

- more detail about schooling and teacher training and about the status of different kinds of universities and the numbers of students catered for;

- whether or not there is any independent academic research on young people and the role, if any, of the HAUK Youth-Public Analytical Centre in this.

In addition, in the course of conversations with young people in Armenia, a request was made for short "a day in the life" accounts describing a typical day for individuals within the very different groups the team met. None, however, were received.

The international review team therefore acknowledges the weaknesses and deficiencies within the body of knowledge it accumulated on youth policy in Armenia.[5] It believes, however, that it succeeded in constructing a sufficiently informed picture to reflect on current aspirations and developments and, in turn, to offer critical feedback that may further assist such progress.

---

4. Former Soviet youth organisations.

5. The international team was asked during the National Hearing whether it felt its information was "enough". It is never enough and there is always more to be sought or explored. An international review, therefore, has to work on the material secured from *a.* the programme of visits made by the international team, *b.* literature provided by the host country, *c.* literature encountered by the team and *d.* additional material provided from unanticipated further sources.

Chapter 2: The international review process

First, it is helpful to provide a brief outline of the international review process. This has evolved over the years since the first review in 1997. Evolution and adjustment have informed both the formal structure of the process and the less formal relationships between international review teams and those within the countries concerned.

The essential model is one in which a prior visit is made to a volunteering country, to determine its rationale for putting itself forward and to establish any significant contemporary concerns relating to its young people (such as educational drop-out or criminality). This preliminary visit, by a senior member of the Directorate of Youth and Sport of the Council of Europe, helps to shape an agenda and a programme of meetings for a first visit. It also helps inform decisions about the composition of the review team, especially the characteristics and specialist knowledge required of the three invited members of the team (who are usually, though not always, established youth researchers), one of whom serves as the rapporteur for the team. The other members of the team are one or more members of the Secretariat of the Council of Europe, and nominees from the two statutory organs of the Directorate of Youth and Sport: the European Steering Group for Youth (CDEJ) and the Advisory Council on Youth, representing youth organisations in Europe.

> - For the review of Armenia, the international review team was composed of the following members:
>
> - Jan Sipos, Slovakia (CDEJ)
>
> - Milosz Czerniejewski, Poland (Advisory Council on Youth)
>
> - Peter Lauritzen (Council of Europe)
>
> - Joanne Hunting (Council of Europe)
>
> - Gavan Titley (youth researcher)
>
> - Ditta Dolejsiova (youth researcher)
>
> - Howard Williamson (youth researcher, rapporteur)

Every review has involved both meetings at the "centre" (with ministries and national organisations) and closer to the ground (with youth projects and regional and local administrations). Ideally, the review team receives a national youth policy report prior to visiting the country, to anchor its understanding and develop positions for further enquiry. This has not always happened and did not in the case of Armenia. With or without a national report, the international team has endeavoured to find useful reference points – such as the European Union White Paper on Youth (European Commission 2001) – to help make sense of and develop an appropriate understanding of a country's youth policy. In the case of Armenia this proved to be particularly inappropriate, and other "markers" had to be found, such as documentation by the United Nations and the World Bank.

It is also important for the review team to be clear about its precise role, for this may differ according to the country concerned. There is, however, always room for misinterpretation, such as assumptions that the team is somehow monitoring performance or judging activity against other countries. In fact, the team is solely concerned with assisting youth policy development and progress, whether through tough criticism or softer advice. Either way, its report and observations are designed to support the country concerned in thinking through ways of addressing weaknesses and building on strengths. The international review team's position is one that could perhaps be best described as "critical complicity": a commitment to a positive and effective youth policy and a desire to work constructively to that end. As one member of the international team in Armenia explained: "This is not a monitoring exercise. We are trying to work from the inside of the country – its feelings, culture, history, challenges." The point was reiterated during another meeting:

> The critical eye of the foreigner has been asked for by Armenia. We are not here to offer a superior eye or to impose European standards. Our job is to understand, and then to provide good examples about programmes, co-operation, approaches and, after the consultations, to help promote a good youth policy for this country.

As well as casting a fresh eye on the national picture of youth policy, the review process allows individual countries to share their knowledge and understanding with other countries, which might benefit from models developed elsewhere. There is also the incremental production of an overall youth policy across Europe: a framework (see Williamson 2002) that may assist in the development of shared standards and approaches. To these ends, the findings of each international review are now presented, both in the host country at a public hearing and to representatives of all 47 member states of the Council of Europe at one of the twice-yearly Joint Council on Youth meetings of the Directorate of Youth and Sport.[6]

The international team visited Armenia on two occasions, in June and November 2005. The first visit was somewhat disorganised and there appeared to be a degree of misunderstanding about what had been agreed and what was required. As a result, considerable time was wasted on unnecessary travel, the absence of interpreters and alterations to the programme. The international review team did not feel that it exploited the full potential of that visit, and it left Yerevan with rather more questions than answers! However, many of these questions were addressed during the second visit, which was organised and managed impeccably by the hosts and allowed the international team to "catch up" considerably. Many thanks are therefore due to the Deputy Minister for Youth Affairs, Lilit Asatryan, and her team, who conferred their hospitality on us.

---

6. Twice a year, at the European Youth Centre either in Strasbourg or Budapest, both the CDEJ and the Advisory Council on Youth (the co-management structure of the Directorate of Youth and Sport) meet both in parallel and then together. At least one international hearing of a youth policy review is usually on the agenda.

Chapter 3: The nation in question

Armenia has a population of just over three million. It is a homogeneous country and over 90% of its citizens are ethnic Armenians, declared members of the Armenian Apostolic Church and speak the Armenian language. There are several small communities of Kurds, Greeks, Russians, Jews and others. Since the Nagorno-Karabakh conflict, Azeris have emigrated from Armenia and Armenians have left Azerbaijan.

With almost 100% of Armenians able to read and write, literacy levels have been impressively high, though there are signs of a small decline. There remains a high commitment to educational participation and achievement, though the links between education and employment have become increasingly tenuous, not least because of the overall demise and transformation of the economy since the implosion of the USSR in 1991. Prior to that, under the old Soviet central planning system, Armenia had developed a modern industrial sector, supplying machine tools, textiles and other manufactured goods to sister republics, in exchange for raw materials and energy (*The World Factbook* 2005). Armenia has few raw materials of its own and experienced severe economic decline in the 1990s, coupled with a chronic energy shortage. It is now, however, a net energy exporter through its nuclear power plant at Metsamor,[7] and has stabilised its economy through a combination of market liberalisation, international aid and foreign direct investment. Armenia remains, nevertheless, a poor country (see below), a situation which is exacerbated by high levels of disability (from the 1988 earthquake and war), military expenditure (6.5% of GDP) and responsibility for refugees (around a quarter of a million from Azerbaijan) and internally displaced persons. For a combination of historical, political, economic and geographical reasons, Armenia faces and experiences distinct challenges concerning the mobility and migration of its people, both within and beyond its borders. It is divided, administratively, into eleven provinces known as *marzpetarans* or *marzes* (a province = a *marz*).

Armenia has existed through centuries of suffering. Its history has frequently been troubled, traumatic and sometimes tragic. Sandwiched between the Tsarist and Ottoman empires before the turn of the 20th century, Armenia achieved a brief but difficult period of independence following the end of the First World War. Without the anticipated support of the victorious western European allies, however, it became absorbed within the emergent Soviet Empire, repeating its earlier absorption into Russia in 1828. By 1920, Armenia's choice was a stark one: between

---

7. Armenia does not have sufficient generating capacity to replace Metsamor nuclear power station, though this is under considerable international pressure to close because it is built on an earthquake fault line.

nationalist Turkey and Soviet Russia. As Hovannisian (2004, p. 304) has observed, "it was in fact no choice at all". The autonomous Republic of Armenia only became a reality once again in 1991, following the collapse of the Soviet Union. This has, however, produced further difficulties and Armenia continues to lean towards Russia for support and connection, despite also wishing to establish and develop its links with Europe and the wider world. The "Russian crisis" of the late 1990s showed just how vulnerable Armenia's dependency can make it: "a decade of economic hardship has worn out the reserves of the population, pointing to the crucial importance of sustained, broad based economic growth" (World Bank 2002, p. 6).

According to at least some of the international NGOs working in Armenia, it is more like a developing country than a transition country – described in a recent report as a "small, resource-poor, landlocked country in the Caucasus" (World Bank 2002, p. 4). This report suggests that, at the end of the last millennium, over half of the population were living in poverty and a quarter in "extreme poverty" (based on the food poverty line). Indeed, World Vision Armenia's 2004 Annual Review, quoting the National Statistical Service of Armenia, confirms a rural poverty rate of 47% and an average monthly income of just US$21.4.

The World Bank report (2002) does, however, detect signs of improvement in the country's socio-economic circumstances, though many of its population remain seriously at risk. While some have benefited from new enterprise and commerce, very low real incomes persist for many and there continues to be a very unequal distribution of wealth, producing "a sharp rise in inequality". Other factors have also contributed to persistent high levels of poverty in Armenia (though there has been some decline in extreme poverty). Limited national resources have meant that expenditure on education has been very low and health care has also deteriorated. The World Bank concludes that more needs to be done to improve the business environment (a range of proposals are made); that more investment is required in education (especially to provide all children with basic education once again); that there needs to be reform and more expenditure on health and that attention needs to be given to maintaining the real value of pensions and means-tested family benefits, and their prompt payment. All these recommendations would contribute significantly to the alleviation of poverty.

The very specific circumstances facing Armenia today, its desperate troubles in the past decade and its long history of struggle for survival, mean that it is virtually impossible to disentangle one issue from another: they are all locked together in response to, and/or as a consequence of, the chaos and conflict that has characterised that history. The position of young people and the construction of youth policy is no exception. Making sense of the purpose of youth policy in Armenia and of the circumstances of young people is not possible without reference to these delicate and difficult episodes throughout the history of Armenia. This includes the recurrent waves of emigration, which mean that the number of Armenians spread throughout the world is three times greater than those in Armenia itself. Money transfers from abroad assist the survival of both the state and individual families and communities. But, even so, some Armenians still choose to leave, at least temporarily, and go to work – both legally and illegally – in other countries, notably Russia and other former member states of the Soviet Union (such as Belarus and Ukraine). They also send remittances home that bolster the local and overall economy. Were it not for these complex, and often rather invisible, economic relationships forged on the anvil of family and social ties over generations, it is difficult to see how Armenia could sustain itself.

There is, perhaps inevitably, something of a siege mentality within Armenia, which produces a particular assertiveness about identity and a commitment to the nation of Armenia and to nation-building. It is important to record this point here, since one of the fundamental tensions and dilemmas for resolution, or at least recognition of its co-existence, is to find a balance between an inward perspective – preoccupied with the problems that directly surround Armenia – and a more outward-looking focus on Armenia's place in Europe. The international review team met people who somehow held both positions comfortably in their heads without acknowledging any sense of contradiction.

Armenia became a member of the Council of Europe in 2001 and has participated in its work ever since. Various monitoring reports on its compliance with the values and standards of the Council of Europe have, however, suggested that Armenia is still falling short in terms of meeting the obligations and commitments to which it signed up in 2004 (Parliamentary Assembly of the Council of Europe 2004a). A report by the International Helsinki Federation for Human Rights (2005) draws attention to a range of human rights violations in relation to, *inter alia*, free and fair elections, media freedoms, peaceful assembly, the independence of the judiciary, arrest and detention, police misconduct, conditions in prisons, religious tolerance, military service and conscientious objection, and the rights of homosexuals. (Many of these issues have direct bearing on the experiences of young people and the framework of youth policy in Armenia.)

Armenia's independent constitution was first adopted by nationwide referendum on 5 July 1995. The international review team's visits to Armenia took place in July and November 2005, shortly before, on 27 November, the constitutional referendum was due to take place. This is the final stage in Armenia's proclaimed intention to fulfil its commitments to the Council of Europe, despite the caveats noted above.

This year, Armenia intends to complete the fulfilment of the implementation of all the commitments undertaken at the country's accession to the Council of Europe. The Council of Europe has expressed its satisfaction with the process of the implementation of Armenia's commitments. The fulfilment of the remaining commitments depends on the introduction of amendments in the Armenian Constitution, for which a referendum is to be conducted this year. The completion of the process of implementation of the Council of Europe's commitments will reaffirm that Armenia is on the irreversible path of constructing a democratic society, based on the rule of law and where human rights are duly respected (Council of Europe Information Office in Armenia 2005, p. 9).

The case for change and development

The above alludes to an "irreversible path" but, in many respects, Armenia remains at a crossroads. Its political and economic situation remains precarious. There is a "frozen" conflict that shows little sign of resolution and a diplomatic stand-off with an adjacent country. This is already producing huge challenges for the integration of Armenia into the global economy. Politically, it seeks to avoid the turbulent, though fortunately not violent, change that has taken place recently both in Ukraine and Georgia: as one respondent put it, "we want to avoid becoming orange or rose; we want to stay yellow".

Both the literature examined and the people the team talked to testify to the persistent dependency "mind-set" of the Armenian people – waiting for something to happen rather that seeking to make things happen. There is, as a result, a stated policy goal of promoting greater participation in civic, economic and political life. Whether or not this is received wisdom and more rhetoric than reality has remained difficult to determine, but the international review team concluded that there appear to be few other options at the moment. This belief guided much of its enquiry and exploration. It was clear, however, that a range of other factors impeded such development. Firstly, the widespread presence of international aid agencies (these were obviously absolutely critical, literally, to the survival of Armenia during the mid-1990s, following war and a profound energy crisis) does promote a sense that help and assistance from outside will remain on hand. Secondly, there has always been a reliance on the Armenian diaspora that has helped to stabilise families and subsidise unemployment. The international review team was told that the diaspora provides over US$1 billion per annum in support of "day-to-day living" as well as capital investment, thus providing support (and theoretically reinforcing a dependency culture) in a different way from international aid NGOs. It should be noted that those US$1 billion also include the allocations of citizens who left for temporary work abroad. Thirdly, it was argued more than once that "employment is not a problem, it is a matter of participation" but, invoking Maslow's Hierarchy of Needs, it is difficult to persuade people to engage more proactively in wider social, economic and political life when they lack the resources for even basic decent living conditions.

The international review team frequently heard the belief expressed that the "light at the end of the tunnel" would be when Armenia became a member of the European Union. Yet this will mean a considerable shift from what is currently a tightly knit "high context" society of strong values, long traditions and commitment to family and religion, to a more disparate "low context" situation of more fluid and flexible beliefs and far greater relativity. Some might not see this as progress but, if it is the direction of travel for Armenia, then there will be sacrifices as well as perceived benefits from engagement with Europe on the long road towards deeper and wider European integration.

Armenia finds itself once again at a crossroads between a democratic future within Europe and the prospect of an inward-looking regime leaning towards the CIS and Russia. There is undoubtedly a willingness to advance along the road towards Europe (Parliamentary Assembly of the Council of Europe 2004b, p. 11).

The international review team learned of the widespread desire for Armenia to open up more to the outside world and to Europe. Young people in particular were eager to engage with the world beyond Armenia's borders – conceptually, virtually and physically. For such aspirations to be realised, there is clearly a need for change and development across political, economic, cultural and legal spheres. The establishment of a coherent, broad-based and opportunity-focused youth policy is one part of that process. What follows is an appraisal of those developments.

Conceptualising "youth"

The political documentation in Armenia clearly defines the term "youth" in the context of state youth policy. They are young people aged between 16 and 30 – citizens of Armenia and some foreign citizens living in Armenia. Youth policy also targets the NGOs that serve them.

In discussion, however, many other age-based definitions of "youth" were put forward, including the 0-18 age group definition of children utilised by the United

Nations Convention on the Rights of the Child and references to young people aged 14 who are permitted to leave school and work if their parents agree to this.

What puzzled the international review team was that it did not hear a more analytical discussion about the concept of "youth". This was surprising as, in Armenia more than in many other countries, there are starker and more striking contrasts in the life course of different groups of young people. Some are in military service both in the border regions and central parts of Armenia while still very young, while others continue with their education well into early adulthood. There appeared to be an absence of "youth sociology" of this kind, which might produce a typology of transitions for Armenian young people. These would include, for example, the male students whose academic learning culminates in a doctorate and who are not constitutionally required to do military service at all. They would also include young women who move rapidly from schooling into married life and motherhood (a transition that is still strongly encouraged in Armenian culture). They would similarly include young people living in rural areas who do not complete their studies and subsequently become unemployed, but are not counted as such in official classifications because they are living "on the land".

Such a sense of short-term and long-term, desired and undesired transition routes, coupled with some idea of their success or failure, would have been helpful to the international team. What happens, for example, to the 3 000 lawyers who qualify each year, or the 10 000 nurses? Are young people defined largely by the fact that they are still in education, or members of the myriad of NGOs which have sprung from student groups? Where do other young people fit in? The international review team had a feeling that "youth" was rather differently conceived in Armenia than elsewhere in Europe, as represented in the youth transitions literature.

Conceptualising "youth policy"

The stated goal of youth policy in Armenia is:

> To provide socio-economic, legal, political, spiritual, cultural and organisational conditions and guarantees for social realisation of the youth and for using their creative power for the benefit of the society most completely (Government of the Republic of Armenia 2005, p. 3).

This broad statement was rendered more concrete by the Deputy Minister for Youth Affairs at the start of the second visit of the international review team:

> Young people are not just consumers any more. The inheritance from the Soviet system was young people simply as consumers, but they can no longer live with the mind-set of their parents (though many still do). Now we have to teach young people to fish, not just to eat the fish. Now there is freedom of speech and youth now have to be active and create their own conditions, not rely on the government. Young people are the policy actors, not policy consumers.

However, the idea of "youth policy", like the ambivalent concept of "youth", lacks clarity in a different way. The international review team detected a kind of "twin track" in the evolution of thinking about youth policy in Armenia. The first dates back to the "Concept on State Youth Policy" of 1998 (see footnote 8) and can still be seen, in a very similar form, in a statement on Youth Policy in Armenia produced by the Ministry of Sport and Youth Affairs in 2005. The second seems to have started much more recently, with a mission report commissioned by UNICEF in 2004 (Denstad and Flessenkemper 2004), subsequently finding its way into government policy as a Youth Policy Strategy for 2005-07, or even 2008![8] (Government of the Republic of Armenia 2005).

The first track outlines the key youth policy areas that are being implemented by the ministry (in the order presented):

- ensuring the protection of the rights of young people;
- provision of youth employment and guarantees relating to their work and implementation of state youth personnel policy;
- supporting the affairs of young people (this is about youth entrepreneurship);
- state assistance to young families;
- provision of guaranteed social services;
- assistance to talented young people;
- formation of the necessary conditions for the spiritual and physical development and civil, patriotic upbringing of young people;
- supporting the activities of youth organisations;
- supporting international collaboration among young people.

This document goes on to describe the range of activities and aspirations in greater detail within a slightly revised framework of "youth policy":

- informative/analytic and youth research;
- leisure, spiritual/physical and patriotic upbringing;
- spiritual/cultural aspects;
- socio-economic side;
- youth NGO activities – co-ordination and development;
- science/education;
- youth co-operation (diaspora, local NGOs, international);
- other activities.

The second track of youth policy – conceptualisation and formulation – has a very different tone and content. Although the document (Government of the Republic of Armenia 2005) initially reiterates much of the content of the *Youth Policy in Armenia* statement, it then moves on to an analysis of the situation of young people in Armenia, framed around four themes: socio-economic aspects, education, health care and citizenship. There are then 14 pages of cogent and powerful analysis of the challenges facing Armenian youth on these fronts. It goes on to set out a youth strategy which, it is argued, has to be embedded within a set of principles linked to participation. Indeed, of the four priorities "of governmental measures for 2005-2007 in the field of governmental youth policy", the very first concerns youth participation:

---

8. The National Report (p. 17) says the strategy is for 2006-07 and expresses rather different objectives from those mentioned above: "the improvement of youth living conditions, organisation of their leisure time and increasing the level of their participation in public, political and civil developments". It also says that the strategy document "was worked out by UNO Children's Fund (Unicef) and approved by the RA Ministry of Culture and Youth Affairs minutes of session six, on February 2, 2006".

- to stimulate participation of young people in society;

- to enhance the employment chances of young people;

- to promote a healthy lifestyle among young people;

- to strengthen the human and institutional capacity of the youth sector and increase knowledge about young people.

In the detailed exposition which follows of what should be included under these headings, there are references to the formation of youth councils, the adoption of the European Charter on the Participation of Young People in Local and Regional Life, the ratification of the European Convention on the Promotion of a Transnational Long-Term Voluntary Service for Young People, a plethora of business advisory and orientation programmes, the need for non-formal education and youth-friendly (sexual) health education and care services.

One should not be surprised at the direction and content of this second document. The consultants commissioned by UNICEF, who produced the report on which this second document is heavily based, were both respected former members of the European Youth Forum. Their advice and recommendations are to be expected (and make sense in view of the evidence presented, though this was also selectively chosen).

What puzzles the international review team is how the two versions of Armenian youth policy are to be reconciled and amalgamated. One (the second) speaks to a modern European agenda, grounded in distinctive, evidence-based challenges facing young people in Armenia and seeing youth not as the problem, but as part of the solution. The other (the first) addresses a different contemporary reality for Armenia: one which still wishes to place emphasis on the family, on producing soldiers and mothers, perhaps (implicitly) on preserving the genetic pool necessary for the survival of Armenian identity. Its twin concerns are with the defence and sustenance of the nation, rather than empowering youth for their own autonomy and self-determination.

Throughout its meetings and deliberations, the international review team recurrently encountered these dual – and in many respects alternative – concepts of youth policy in Armenia. Those the team spoke to invariably started by projecting the more progressive, somewhat idealistic, second version but then had a tendency to fall back on the more grounded and pragmatic version – one which is probably better understood by most of them and closer to their hearts.

A further version of the objectives of youth policy in Armenia, giving primacy to both nation-building and youth participation, is outlined in the National Report (p. 24): "to create national and common to all mankind values, responsibilities for motherland and nation deep awareness development among young people, legislative, economical and organisational conditions and guarantees for self-orientation and self-assertion".

Delivery of youth policy – structures and finance

Legislative framework

State youth policy of the Republic of Armenia, which is one of the most important functions of the state, has strategic importance. It aims at providing legal, economic and administrative conditions and guarantees for comprehensive development, self-realisation and self-expression of the young generation, conscious of national and universal values and having a deep understanding and feeling of responsibility towards their motherland and own people, with the ultimate goal of ensuring political, socio-economic and cultural development of the Republic of Armenia (Government of the Republic of Armenia 2004, p. 3).

The state youth policy of the Republic of Armenia, which is one of the most important governmental activities, has strategic importance here. It should be aimed at creating legal, economic and organisational conditions and guarantees for all-round development of young people who would have access to the values common to all mankind and to the national ones, who realize deeply their responsibility before the motherland and Armenian people (Government of the Republic of Armenia 2005, p. 2).

Both of these quotations are included here, since they reflect the gradual refinement of the principles and framework of youth policy over time, as Armenia moves towards establishing a youth law. Immediately after the second quotation above, it is asserted that "the sphere of youth strategy has been shaped in the country today", and the strategy then states, significantly, that "youth NGOs are the most organised entities of the state youth policy and they always should be the carriers of the state youth policy and basic means of its implementation" (Government of the Republic of Armenia 2005, p. 2). It was within this framework that the international review team sought to explore the principles, policy and practice of Armenia's evolving strategic thinking in relation to its young people.

At the time of the international review there was still no youth law, though one had been tried and rejected in 2002 and another was apparently in process. By the end of 2005, the draft of the Law on State Youth Policy had been approved by the Government of the Republic of Armenia and was waiting to be ratified by the National Assembly (Parliament). That youth law has been almost a decade in the making, starting with a state youth policy concept or conception[9] in 1998, which determined "the basic provisions and directions based on which the State Youth Policy of Armenia is developed and implemented". Reference is made elsewhere in this text to those documents, since the broad framework concerning the subjects of state youth policy, its principles and its primary areas of focus have remained substantively unchanged. Significantly, its fourth section, entitled "Priority Measures Necessary for the Implementation of State Youth Policy", identifies three critical issues:

- the creation of a legislative framework for the efficient implementation of state youth policy;

- the development and implementation of integrated and targeted youth-related programmes, as well as integration of youth problems into environmental, social, cultural and economic state programmes;

- the establishment of an appropriate state infrastructure (youth centres, information/analysis centres at national and regional level, youth funds and so on) for the efficient implementation of youth policy (Government of the Republic of Armenia 1998b, p. 4).

---

9. The international review team received two slightly different documents, one entitled "Concept on State Youth Policy", the other "Conception of State Youth Policy", both produced in 1998. The cover of the latter also states "Adopted by the Government of Republic of Armenia, Yerevan, 1998". There is little difference between them, apart from the occasional substitution of different words, such as "aim" instead of "direction", and "formation" instead of "creation". One wonders quite why such words were changed! The State Youth Policy conception established by RA Government decree No. 789 as of 14 December 1998 remains, however, "the first and yet the only legal normative document, by regulations of which the RA State Youth Policy is directed" (National Report, p. 20).

Clearly, as this report indicates, all three are not just desirable requirements but essential components of an effective youth policy.[10]

Finance

There is, perhaps inevitably given the economic challenges facing Armenia, a huge gap between the aspirations of youth policy and the capacity of the government to resource them. The state budget, for a population of three million people, was said to be not much more than €400m,[11] though it was claimed that this "would increase dramatically over the next few years". Just 1% of the state budget is for youth issues. (It should be noted, however, that direct budget allocations for youth programmes have risen 1054% since 1997 (National Report, p. 21). Indeed, the reason the first draft youth law in 2002 was rejected at its second reading was because it made excessive social commitments in the context of the existing budget. It was simply not deliverable. The current proposed youth law is declarative – a statement of aspirations and intentions – and sits alongside other legislation in employment, housing, volunteering and welfare, which have a more direct impact on young people. The value of the new law, if passed, is that it would have more authority than a government decree.

The annual budget of the Youth Policy Department within the Ministry of Sport and Youth Affairs is around €450 000, of which two thirds (€300 000) is for distribution to NGOs through the Centre for Organising Youth Events (see below). A further €40 000 was raised by the ministry in 2004 from various international organisations, but this was still insufficient to deliver all its strategic intentions. The youth strategy will, it was conceded, have to be adjusted according to the resources available. This may be the reality but there is, equally, a debate to be had over whether or not stringent resources – the constant anxiety over sufficient finance – impede the construction of an overarching vision of what young people in Armenia need. The point was well made by Denstad and Flessenkemper in their observation of the workshop they held as part of their mission to develop a youth strategy in Armenia:

> At times, one could have the impression that participants had no idea what was needed to be undertaken to improve the situation of young people. Participants were not able to discuss issues at the strategy level, but almost immediately jumped into specific activities or suggested legislative projects (Denstad and Flessenkemper 2004, p. 2).

Neither recourse to legislation, nor commitment to practical projects, nor even financial resources are, ultimately, what is needed for youth policy developments. These have to flow from a shared national commitment to a vision and, as noted above, that vision could be argued to be a varied and partial one, subject to very different levels of loyalty from those involved in the youth policy field.

---

10. It was argued by some, however, that real and important youth policy lay outside official "youth policy" in the areas of education, family and marriage. Laws were being passed in these areas, based on European standards. And though laws alone could not solve problems, they did provide a "clarity flow"!

11. Wales, albeit part of the United Kingdom, has a delegated budget for "devolved functions" (i.e. not including defence, criminal justice, taxation and so on). That budget, for three million people, is around €18 billion – over 40 times greater than that of Armenia, with fewer commitments! Another parallel would be Slovenia, with a population of two million people, where the state budget is in the region of €800 million – double that of Armenia, though still relatively modest by western European standards, for two thirds of the people.

Structures for delivery

Vertical delivery

At the heart of the endeavour to turn the vision for youth policy in Armenia into a reality lies the Ministry of Sport and Youth Affairs of the Republic of Armenia. Within the ministry is a Youth Policy Department (established in 1995, now with seven specialist staff but, critically, led by a dedicated "youth minister", a deputy minister within the ministry).

The Ministry of Sport and Youth Affairs, therefore, through the Youth Policy Department, was described as the government's "agent" for carrying out youth policy. The specific functions of the department are to:

- propose legislation;

- make amendments;

- provide strategic advice to government;

- carry out projects;

- support training;

- promote international projects for international co-operation;

- establish memoranda of understanding with counterparts elsewhere;

- liaise with ministers and deputy ministers;

- engage in practice through the Centre for Organising Youth Events;

- collect and analyse information on young people.

The state youth policy of the Government of the Republic of Armenia, the international review team was told, enjoys the close and increasing attention of the president, given the "big challenges faced by the government in relation to young people in Armenia". The deputy minister herself suggested that youth policy development and delivery fell into two distinct stages – the first (between 1997 and 2002) was "just starting", the second (since 2003) was attempting to "advance and strengthen" cross-ministry co-ordination and to establish regional and local youth councils: "the National Youth Council can't deal with the more local issues, so we intend to develop similar councils within the regions and localities".

Also linked to the Youth Policy Department is the Centre for Organising Youth Events, a non-commercial state organisation, established by government decree in 2002. The centre now has some 18 staff, whose responsibility is to decide upon grant allocations to NGOs and the programmes and projects they are pursuing. This process was outlined to the international review team by one director of an NGO:

> First of all you have to be registered with the ministry, which happens after you have completed a detailed questionnaire. Then you can apply and the application is reviewed by a Reviewing Committee in the Ministry of Sport and Youth Affairs, then it goes to the Finance Ministry to review the budget, and then it goes to a third committee in the Centre for Organising Youth Events – and, if it gets past all these, then they sign an agreement with you and the money is released and you report back to the Youth Events committee.

That particular organisation received under US$10 000 in 2004, though the grant received financed two particular projects. (Resources can stretch quite a long way in Armenia – a point it is important to remember.) The centre is also responsible for fund-raising from non-governmental and international sources, commercial activities and youth-related information. Some of the centre's staff are physically located within the ministry, thus ensuring close dialogue and co-ordination.

The direct lines for the delivery of state youth policy are therefore as follows:

Structures Implementing the State Youth Policy and Policy-Related Non-Governmental Organisations and Foundations in the Republic of Armenia

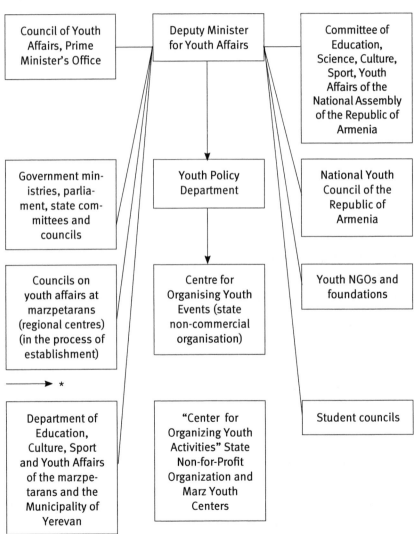

* The National Report (p. 24) includes this diagram, but adds, where the arrow is, the "All-Armenian International Youth Centre" Fund, about which the international team received little information; see also National Report, p. 21, footnote 2.

The impression received by the international review team was that while there is quite a lot going on at the centre and in the capital, there is only a limited sense of regional or local governance of youth policy and youth issues. The ministry itself acknowledged that regional centres were only now being established and the team was told that there was, routinely, only one person in the regions responsible for youth issues and no-one designated to that task at more local levels (for example, in the villages). More than once, it was noted that although Armenia now has a progressive legal system (the 1999 law requiring education for all was often cited), there are still few mechanisms for implementation and even fewer for enforcing the law. As a result, often very little happened.

The international review team remained unclear about the specific responsibilities of those working within the Youth Policy Department and concluded that the primary path in the delivery of youth policy was through programmes provided by youth NGOs – subject to sufficient funding, some of which was available through the ministry (see below). For example, the Memorandum of Understanding between the ministry and World Vision Armenia made provision for co-operation in the realms of supporting children with special needs "after they reach adolescence", participation and the involvement of the public ("with a special emphasis on youth") and the provision of "informal education courses" (World Vision Armenia 2005, p. 1).

The international review team also failed to find out what had happened to the network of buildings that had been available to young people under communism. In many former communist countries, these had typically disappeared in the "wild west" environment that followed the collapse of communism, but in some countries they had been retained for use by young people under new arrangements. Some such buildings in Armenia, the team was told, were being used by the church and village communities for leisure and non-formal educational activity, but no-one provided any evidence of the scale and nature of such provision, or any detailed account of its usage by young people.[12]

The impression the team gained is that the likelihood of good ideas being put into practice is very much contingent on individual persistence and motivation, though clearly those with greater institutional, political and resource back-up are at an advantage. Many talented Armenians seem to go abroad for a while but then come back. They face the challenge of working in a more adverse environment but are accorded considerable respect for attempting to do so. As one such individual commented:

> I have a lot of friends with skills who went abroad and they also came back. We are the social security for our families. And perhaps there is also the status of being here. And everything is just developing here and so is more challenging. Lower salary, more headaches, longer hours, working weekends! But it is interesting. I enjoy working in the nongovernmental, non-commercial sector.

The deputy minister was equally buoyant in her commitment, suggesting that the next steps in youth policy delivery were:

- the government to accept the Youth Law;
- to secure acceptance of the youth strategy;

---

12. During the visit for the National Hearing, the international team learned that the pan-Armenian Youth Centre was based in a former Komsomol building, though many people mistakenly thought that it was newly built.

- to establish the regional youth councils in the *marzpetarans*;[13]

- to join the Partial Agreement on the Youth Card;

- to explore other European initiatives in order to bring back best practice.

Horizontal delivery

> Youth is a cross-ministry issue and responsibility, and the Deputy Minister for Youth has full authority, though if you were sending a letter to another minister, it would go through the Minister of Culture.

There is clearly a prevailing view, from many quarters, that youth policy in Armenia remains fragmented and unco-ordinated, though those who advanced this view also acknowledged how much better things had become through the energy and commitment of the Deputy Minister for Youth Affairs.[14] She had "pulled things much closer together", at least at the level of government and national pro- grammes. It was noted that Armenia was not alone in not having a government willing or able to step forward and co-ordinate international NGO activity, though this was now very much needed. After all, the independent Armenian government had relatively little experience of this kind of relationship and, furthermore, many NGOs did not want to be restricted, preferring instead to pursue their own priorities and objectives, which tended to derive from their experts' reports. International NGOs, it was felt, often worked with different government ministries in different ways, and they also supported national NGOs, including youth NGOs. There were, it was alleged, rather too many "suitcase" international bodies, disbursing funds in a somewhat scattergun fashion. On many occasions it was suggested that youth NGOs were not formed to pursue issues or interests but to get grants (see below).

Although there were some cynical remarks ("there is clear evidence of intentional non-co-ordination"), most respondents pointed to developments that they regarded as significant in contributing to a more coherent approach to youth pol- icy: the status of youth NGOs, the youth ministry's website, the youth newspaper, youth councils, and a growing awareness of the youth field and youth issues. Indeed, criticisms that "very little is joined up, integrated, or cross-sectoral" were tempered by recognition that there had been "reasonably significant develop- ments in just two years, within a culture that appears resistant to change". At a municipal level, efforts were being made to co-ordinate the work of youth NGOs

---

13. The establishment of regional youth centres is described as an "unprecedented programme" in the National Report (p. 18). They will be the regional representatives of the Centre for Organising Youth Events, in collaboration with local self-governmental bodies, regional public and international organisations. Their objective is "to make the State Youth Policy available for regional youth, efficiently involve them into the programs, raise the level of awareness about youth policy. The regional youth centers will be governed by the management councils formulated by the representatives of the above-mentioned organisations. The youth centers will act as recourse (sic) centers, where young people will have opportunities to use different services necessary for them (legislative and health councils, computer service, library, reading room), get knowledge through organized classes, professional orientation, and productively organize their leisure" (National Report, p. 18). The youth centres will be established in the regions of Lori, Shirak, Sjunik, Tavush, Gegharquniq, Vajots Dzor, Aragatsotn, Kotajk, Ararat and Armavir (National Report, p. 144). In parallel, there is the creation of councils on youth affairs for the *marzpetarans*, designed to promote the inclusion and participation of young people (National Report, p. 25).

14. Between the international team's visits and the National Hearing, the post of Deputy Minister for Youth changed hands. During the National Hearing visit, the new deputy minister contested this allegation that youth policy was "fragmented and unco-ordinated". The response of the international review team was that this was a widespread perception, but it would be quite willing to register the deputy minister's posi- tion as well.

and to establish a regional council, following consultations with young people through a youth conference. Such horizontal co-ordination at the regional level of the *marz* is not only important for itself but also in terms of relating national policy to local government.

Structural questions

Recommendations:

The international team feels that such developments need to be consolidated and developed. This is likely to be best achieved through a more formalised cross-ministry structure (an inter-ministerial committee/group on youth affairs), stronger governmental co-ordination of the work of international NGOs and a more formalised network of national youth NGOs. Bringing each of these "levels" to the same table would, over time, help to inform a more robust and connected youth strategy for Armenia, which, in itself, would build up the existing Youth Policy Strategy and aspirations to deliver it through the development of regional youth centres. Regional youth strategies could ensure the achievement of national strategy objectives through the engagement of relevant national youth NGOs at the regional level.

Youth organisations

The mission of the organisation is: to develop a new generation of highly professional lawyers, who have new modes of thinking and will promote to the establishment of the rule of law, democracy and the formation of civil society in Armenia, where the people are aware of their rights and their rights are protected (Armenian Young Lawyers Association 2003, p. 7).

The Armenian Young Lawyers Association (AYLA) was founded by a group of law students in 1995, with the aim of supporting a new generation of lawyers in advancing Armenia as a sovereign, democratic, legal and social state. AYLA claims to be one of the most recognised youth NGOs in Armenia and one that commands considerable trust. It engages in a range of activities (including free advocacy for vulnerable social groups) and is well connected internationally. It is not typical of many other youth NGOs which are as often, or more often, donor-driven and only active when donor finance permits, rather than constructed on a clear set of values and principles and a defined mission and developed in response to identified and evidenced need, as AYLA is.

The activities of NGOs in Armenia were reinvigorated following independence from the Soviet Union. They are regulated by the Law on Non-Governmental Organisations, adopted on 4 December 2001 (National Report, p. 112). There are around 4 000 NGOs registered with the Ministry of Justice.[15] About half of NGOs are either specifically youth NGOs or they deal with youth issues, though many do not function actively.

A recurrent concern expressed was that while many NGOs were focused on important themes – such as social activities, human rights, environment, women's issues, refugees, people with disabilities, education and young people – the rules

---

15. This is according to the National Report, p. 113. The State Youth Policy Strategy, p.18, says there are "about 3 000". This figure was repeated in discussions, where it was suggested that only about 10% were youth organisations, and many of these were hardly active: "one man shows, or just for projects".

governing their existence are restrictive and stifling of initiative. This was disputed by government officials, who felt that NGO laws were "quite open and transparent", but many others said that NGOs were trapped by rules, regulations and patronage, and especially by the law forbidding NGOs to conduct business activities, which means that they cannot raise funds through commercial measures.

Youth organisations were said to be rather weak and "not consistent with international standards" in Armenia. The government, it was alleged, exerted too much control over them. As the international team discovered on other fronts, there appeared to be a lack of transparency and trust between NGOs and the government, though things appeared to have improved considerably since the Deputy Minister for Youth Affairs analysed the structure and function of youth NGOs in Armenia, prior to implementing a new approach to delivering the support they needed. The transparency of that approach seems to have been welcomed by many youth NGOs, though perhaps the most vocal support came from beneficiaries.

More significant is the apparent lack of trust in youth NGOs and limited involvement in them on the part of the vast majority of young people. Though NGOs may have a value to those involved, only 7.2% of young people in the national report survey trusted NGOs (National Report, p. 113). The National Report suggests that youth NGOs are playing a decreasing role in the lives of young people and is explicit in suggesting that youth NGOs should be much more active in:

- delivering youth programmes;
- co-ordinating volunteering activity;
- forging coalitions;
- leading campaigns.

Once again, it has to be recognised that youth NGOs in Armenia are still on a sharp learning curve, endeavouring to position themselves between being, what an Australian researcher once described as, heads of a movement or arms of the state.

The National Report points to the critical contribution made by student organisations to youth policy in Armenia:

> The development and activity of student organisations played a great role in influencing the establishment of youth policy in Armenia. Preceding the formation of a youth NGO-sector they proved an actual incentive in the sphere of "organized youth". Until 2000-01 many important actors in the youth sphere of both state and social sectors were the building blocks in the formation and development of student entities in different state institutions of higher education (National Report, p. 117).

Though such activism appears to be in decline, this point should not be forgotten, nor the fact that "student bodies played a great and in some ways a decisive role in the foundation of the Armenian National Youth Council (1997)" (National Report, p. 121). The international team met students from the Student Confederation of Yerevan State University and learned a great deal about its activities, energy, interests, focus and service. The National Report (p. 119) notes, however, that "the wide masses of students are not sufficiently motivated to get involved in the activities of self-governed student bodies and do not see SCs [student councils] as protectors of their interests".

Nevertheless, despite this proclaimed widespread apathy and mistrust among young people, including students, Armenia has made concerted efforts to establish and support a range of youth councils.[16] Indeed, there is a youth council linked to the parliament and one to the prime minister's office; there is a youth council in Yerevan under the mayor's office and there are emergent regional youth councils, following a decision to set them up at a youth seminar in 2003. Inevitably, it is argued that these assist contact, co-ordination, the exchange of information and the identification of shared areas of interests. Others, including the international team for some time, feel confused about their relationship and respective roles. The youth council related to parliament is constituted through representatives of student councils and other youth organisations. It can advise on legislation that may affect young people – but so does the youth council linked to the prime minister! Regional youth councils are composed both of representatives of youth organisations and independent (self-determined) members. The government has initiated an award for young people who have made an active contribution to this development.

The Armenian National Youth Council became a member of the European Youth Forum in November 2005. Within Armenia, it contributes – as part of the expert council – to decisions about the disbursement of government resources to youth NGOs for projects and programmes.

Despite discussions with a number of national youth NGOs, representatives of the National Youth Council and government officials, the international team felt it still had more questions than answers. There appeared to be something of an inner circle of more privileged youth NGOs, that were almost as much part of government as independent from it, and that certainly benefited from government patronage and financial support. The understanding of a genuine civil society appeared to remain elusive.

Youth organisations and youth structures

Recommendations:

The international review team applauds the efforts being made in Armenia to promote and support youth NGOs and youth structures, in a variety of ways and at a range of levels. However, though much progress has been made in a relatively short time, there is clearly a long way to go in terms of compliance with international standards and concepts. Most significantly, it is important for "civil society" to be understood as self-organised and to be separated from the state. More concretely, there needs to be a more robust communication strategy to ensure that young people know what is available to them and why their engagement and contribution is important. Youth organisations themselves will have to direct more energy and effort to persuading young people that they are trustworthy and attractive. The National Youth Council should consider dispelling external perceptions that it is too closed a "club", by reflecting on its criteria for membership, mechanisms for appointment, contact with member organisations and frequency and location of meetings. It might wish to think about an annual general assembly. The government also needs to establish a more robust strategy for enabling and ensuring youth participation not just through hierarchies of youth councils but through involvement in decision-making across structures of governance.

---

16. Though very little indeed is said about this in the National Report.

Chapter 4: The young people the team met

Apart from the students at Yerevan University and the young people who were involved in professional meetings, the international review team was fortunate to meet two groups of "ordinary" children and young people, who revealed how they spent their lives and anticipated their futures.

Both groups suggested that their time was always occupied, largely through studying and partly through purposeful leisure activity, especially sports. They had no time, they said, for casual play! About a third made use of the Internet, which is consistent with findings presented in the National Report. Few, however, had travelled outside Armenia and then only to Georgia and Russia (admittedly many were under the age of 16, whereas the National Report (p. 43) indicates that some 29% of young people over the age of 16 have been abroad).

The young people held great hopes that diligent study would enable them to go to university and that university qualifications would help them to achieve their occupational aspirations, which were very varied: music, design, engineering and medicine. Virtually all the young people said that they would like to travel in the future, though they remained attached and committed to the traditions of their homeland. Going to church was "part of our life". Their musical preferences incorporated Armenian, Russian and Western styles.

They appeared relaxed about their current lifestyles, though all said that despite being very occupied – and preoccupied – with studying, they would like a wider choice of leisure and entertainment options, especially a cinema. This seemed to be part of a general desire to have more access to, and contact with, the wider world – to share understanding of different life experiences.

Few of the young people were confident, and a number expressed deep uncertainty, about the future. Most of them worried about their ability to earn enough money; one commented: "I have no guarantee of positive things happening to me in the future." This was why they were all so committed to their studies – to strengthen the probability of securing a more certain future. But, as one of them said, this focus on studying also had the effect of narrowing their development:

> Personally I think it is not so good to concentrate only on studies. I don't think it is needed to paint life in just one colour. We need to be involved in different things.

-----> **Dimensions of "youth policy"— key domains of youth policy**

i. Education, training and employment

The young people the team met were convinced that investment in learning would translate into better employment prospects, consistent with their aspirations. Yet virtually all those professionals who commented on education and the labour market in Armenia said that a radical overhaul was urgently required, and that this was only just starting to be effected. As the National Report (p. 56) observes:

> The development of the RA educational system in the present phase is closely bound to the international trends of public development which, in their turn, are conditioned by the irreversible changes taking place in the global economy.

Elsewhere in the National Report (p. 63), this point is reinforced:

> Substantial changes and reforms in education are of critical importance as at present it is a top priority to educate a generation ready to meet the challenges of the future.
>
> In this respect it is essential not only to convey the knowledge to students but, at the same time, to shape an informed and involved citizen capable of making decisions.

This second quotation captures the challenge in Armenia to construct an education system that not only connects more closely to changing labour market demands and needs, but also supports the cultivation of greater initiative and self-direction amongst young people, in order to foster participation in civil society and exercise of more widespread entrepreneurship.

Time and again, the "dependency culture" in Armenia was mentioned. This was attributed firmly to Soviet traditions, within which the Armenian economy flourished by complementing industry and commerce in other parts of the Soviet Union.[17] Occupational destinations were guaranteed, according to levels of educational achievement. Making the transition from the old planned Soviet economy to a market economy has proved to be extremely painful, exacerbated by the energy crisis of the early 1990s, conflict with Azerbaijan and the blockade with Turkey.[18]

The National Report provides a good descriptive account of the structure of general, professional and higher education in Armenia. Here, therefore, this report will only identify some of the more salient challenges in the provision of both formal and non-formal education, vocational training and the labour market. It is important, however, to emphasise that these are all inter-related, or should be. The overall challenge for Armenia is to re-connect these relationships in the context of a changing society and economy.

Formal education

Virtually all children in Armenia start their formal education at the age of 7 (though this will soon reduce to 5 or 6) and move through to the eighth grade of general education. Some children do drop out, though this is very rare, although the State Youth Policy Strategy reports that some 6-7% of children aged 7-16, notably girls, do not attend school.

---

17. In 1991 there were 890 factories in Armenia of which 600 were dealing with chemical production – dirty and dangerous work, with no complete product "in order to stay subordinate to Moscow". Only three medicines were partially produced; now more than 100 are completely produced.

18. The international team was told that a report to the European Parliament had suggested that US$5 million of trade is lost because of the blockade with Turkey.

The international team heard a considerable amount of discussion about the education of young people with disabilities: indeed, disability in general seemed to be a significant item on many agendas (see below). The team learned that, historically, children with disabilities had been completely segregated from other children, but that there were now a number of integration initiatives, including training teachers to work with children with physical disabilities. There were still special schools (around ten) for children with more profound learning disabilities. Within and beyond schooling, however, aspirations for the greater integration of people with disabilities were often obstructed by the design of buildings. There was, for example, no wheelchair access.

At the level of higher education, it was conceded that behind the impressive figures (such as the fact that Armenia has some 70 private universities and 20 state universities[19]), there were major questions about standards, quality and relevance. Armenia is a signatory to both the Lisbon Process and the Bologna Declaration[20] (signed in May 2005), and is therefore committed to significant educational reform. Part of the Bologna Declaration, for example, requires at least 70% of students leaving higher education to be working in the profession for which they have been educated. Currently, only the American University in Armenia would comply with this standard. It was observed repeatedly that too many students were training for professions that were not in sufficient demand in the labour market. Lawyers and nurses, trained in their thousands in Armenia, were often used to illustrate this point, though it was also noted that many went to work abroad or, in the case of women, had children and ceased to work.

The fundamental concern of the international review team was the content of learning throughout an individual's education. Clearly young people in Armenia learn a lot and there is a huge cultural commitment to education. Yet encyclopaedic knowledge does not transfer to a capacity to reflect on, question, analyse and distil material within the context of particular aims or frameworks. This latter kind of aptitude, one which is thought to be more essential for learning societies and global economies,[21] appears to remain relatively subordinated within Armenian learning culture. After all (the question was asked rhetorically), how can someone learn economics for five years and still have little idea about the practicalities of setting up their own business? There still appears to be a firmly traditional pedagogy, one in which the teacher transmits knowledge, rather than one in which learners develop understanding. The latter "learner-centred" approach relates significantly to the practice of non-formal education (see below), but is also, increasingly, a dimension of formal education in many countries.

The National Report indicates firmly that major educational reforms are now in progress. It does appear to the international review team that these are a critical

---

19. Some of the private universities are accredited by the state; others are not. The credibility of non-accredited universities is declining, though they are cheaper to study at and therefore still attractive to some young people. For the future, however, it was suggested that the competition will be between state and accredited private universities; non-accredited "universities" will die out or re-focus their provision to lower level, more vocational learning.

20. Concern was expressed at the National Hearing that the Bologna Process and the greater mobility thus permitted for "highly qualified specialists" might have the adverse effect of exacerbating the "brain drain" from Armenia.

21. A group of very bright students in Prague in 1999 came up with the "learning requirements" in conditions of globalisation. This they summed up as "FREUD in a human envelope": educators needed to support young people in developing – within the proliferation of information available through the Internet and elsewhere – a capacity to Find, Retrieve, Evaluate, Use and Defend whatever they chose to make use of.

element of a process whereby Armenia can move from being – in at least some ways – a rather closed society (in both geographical and intellectual terms) to one which seeks to broaden its horizons towards Europe and open up both its intellectual and, in time, geographical borders.

Non-formal education

It was surprising how frequently the international team was told that non-formal education was of paramount importance in Armenia. It is, of course, a central element of the State Youth Policy Strategy ("one of the priorities"), though it was acknowledged that, apart from the Ministry of Sport and Youth Affairs, there was little input on this front from the government and it was left largely to international NGOs. Other people, it was conceded, "are not really aware or interested in this".

The State Youth Policy Strategy accepts that a system of non-formal education is "a rather new phenomenon", but that the challenges faced by the young people of Armenia cannot be solved without a creative approach, flexibility and personal responsibility. These attributes can be engendered through non-formal education: "one of the main methods promoting participation, activeness and social integration of youth."

Establishing a robust platform for the development of non-formal learning opportunities is, however, proving rather difficult. The National Report (p. 70) suggests that non-formal education "is considered to be one of the foundation stones of youth policy" and that an important measure of youth policy "is how the Government enhances the active educational processes outside the formal education system". Yet the culture of the formal education system inhibits acceptance of other approaches. Notwithstanding the fact that most young people in Armenia have never heard of the concept – and that even the small minority who have generally cannot describe what it is[22] – the applied methods invoked are fundamentally alien. Young people:

> draw a clear line of distinction between roles (teacher and learner), often consider the proposed exercises not serious and ridiculous. This is a consequence of formal (academic) education approaches, which almost exclude interactive methods, or, for example, simulation exercises (Markosyan et al. 2002, quoted in the National Report, p. 71).

In order to redress this situation, the Ministry of Labour and Social Issues is in the process of preparing a concept paper on non-formal education, outlining its rationale, purpose and application.

It was suggested that the reason the idea of non-formal education was mentioned so frequently to the international team was because it was one of the easiest ways to get grants – in order to carry out "training" through non-formal education – which, in turn, sustained the existence and survival of many youth NGOs (see above). During the first visit of the international team, only one youth NGO described its provision with more specificity: the use of non-formal education was in parallel with formal education – a supplement, not a substitute. It was about "building confidence and initiative, not just about filling their heads and then locking the ideas in"! During the second visit, however, the international team met with a number of other youth NGOs. It was clear that there was some groundswell in the promotion of non-formal education, even within the domain of professional and

---

22. Those who can have invariably attended training courses run by the Council of Europe at one of the European Youth Centres in either Strasbourg or Budapest.

youth policy in Armenia

vocational studies, where work was being done with schools and colleges and in sectors such as hairdressing, clothes design and computing. These NGOs were clearly part of a network that was advancing the cause of, and case for, non-formal education in Armenia (see Markosyan et al. 2002).

Vocational training

The international team struggled to make sense of the scale and form of vocational training provision. It learned that there used to be vocational schools that prepared technicians for working in Soviet enterprises, but these had mainly collapsed after 1989. Some new vocational schools had been created and the private non-accredited "universities" also offered vocational preparation (in sectors such as hairdressing).

The problem lay not just in provision but also in demand for such courses. Young people in Armenia invariably wanted higher education qualifications and more learning. This was certainly what the team found in their discussions with young people.[23]

The team was told that education is valued almost above all else in Armenian culture. As a result, parents and families will do "almost anything" to support their children in getting a university education. So, although the team was told that young people from the regions often came from poor families and could not afford a university education, they were also told that families and young people themselves stretched their resources to the limit to support such study. The minimum salary had improved, from €5-6 a month a few years ago, to an average wage of around €150 a month. Many families received support from relatives abroad, and young people today were also willing to "work in a gas station or as a waiter" to finance their studies, whereas in the past they were not.

There is, therefore, both a cultural and labour market challenge regarding vocational preparation and training.[24] Though there have been training programmes established by the government, 90% of young people do not seem to be aware of them. The 2003 Poverty Reduction Strategy Programme suggests that even those who take up such programmes are not successful (in the sense that they do not get a sustainable job afterwards) for a number of reasons:

- employers do not honour their promises to recruit trainees (they do so for a month but no more);

- the training provided is not relevant to the market;

23. Though the international team asked for figures, these were not provided. The State Youth Policy Strategy, drawing on a 2002 education, poverty and economic activities survey, reports that just under half of young people do not continue their education after graduation from school because of an absence of financial means. However, the country's authorities indicated that on 1 September 2005, the number of students enrolled in public and private education establishments was 97 765, and that in accordance with 2005 official statistics, the number of young people was 821 600, meaning that only 11.9% were participating in higher education.

24. This is not unique to Armenia! In many countries there is not "parity of esteem" between vocational and academic learning, despite repeated and concerted efforts to achieve it. Moreover, there is often a fundamental misunderstanding of vocational training – a view that it is simply and solely concerned with practical competencies. In fact, in many vocational areas, there is an increasing need for a repertoire of interpersonal and social skills as "service" expectations increase – not just in developing sectors such as tourism and hospitality, but also in more traditional sectors such as plumbing and construction. Thus there is a growing overlap between the knowledge, skills and attitudes that have traditionally been linked to particular forms of academic, vocational and non-formal education and learning.

- the time available is not enough to train people properly;
- too many people are training, producing a surplus.

Nevertheless, in response to labour market demand for skills in new technologies, the Ministry of Sport and Youth Affairs is organising computer training and technology specialisation – involving mainly young people – throughout the country.

Labour market

The mismatch between learning by young people and labour market demand manifests itself in high levels of youth unemployment, or the employment of young people in sectors and at levels that are not commensurate with their qualifications. Some sectors (such as the law) are saturated; other sectors (such as new technologies) are unable to recruit sufficiently skilled young people.

Labour market statistics in any country are notoriously difficult to interpret, and Armenia is no exception. Unravelling the numerous statistics provided concerning both participation and non-participation of young people in the labour market proved to be almost impossible. Indeed, the National Report (p. 30) indicates that although just 4% of young people (34 000[25]) are registered as unemployed with the employment services, 22% of the young people in its specially commissioned survey declared that they were without work. There are suggestions that unemployment has decreased in recent years (and evidence of an upturn in the economy, from a stagnant position to 10-13% growth, according to the National Report, p. 28), but there is also evidence of a decrease in taxpayers! It was often difficult for the international team to "square the circle" between claims of very high levels of unregistered unemployment and parallel claims of enormous participation in higher education – if so many are in education, then there is unlikely to be so much youth unemployment.

Few people challenged the view that levels of real employment may well be underestimated, and that levels of real unemployment are definitely underestimated. There are few incentives for young people to register as unemployed, for unemployment benefits are available only to people who have worked for over one year.[26] It was also suggested, on many occasions, that there is a shadow economy in Armenia comprising perhaps as much as 30% of the employed workforce. The National Report (p. 31) says that "non-formal employment has quickly widened and strengthened".

Young people in Armenia appear to be deeply suspicious of public employment services. Even if they choose to register as unemployed, registration is a bureaucratic nightmare. Should they be offered a job, even at the minimum wage of US$30 a month, then they are no longer considered unemployed but "unwilling to work". Alternatively, they may be required to undertake service in the community in return for state benefits, and indeed many young people are on such programmes. Given such distrust in public services, a host of private training and orientation services have been established, and one fifth of the young people in

---

25. This nevertheless constitutes 28% of the total number of registered unemployed.
26. Only about one third of young people had even heard of the State Employment Service, according to the survey conducted for the National Report (p. 31). The National Report (p. 29) also draws attention to the fact that "employment" is very broadly defined – to include students and those doing military service – and may even include "numerous unemployed people", such as those living on farms in the countryside: "such problems … may have great influence on the statistic picture."

the National Report survey had made use of them, though another fifth expressed no trust in these services either (National Report, p. 33).

The government is very keen to promote more enterprise and self-employment. Beyond overcoming barriers to do with the alleged "dependency culture" among young people in Armenia, the National Report (p. 34) claims that although two thirds of young people in its survey expressed a wish to have their own business, there were perceived barriers to achieving this, such as financial problems, taxes, duties and corruption. Nevertheless, in partnership with the International Labour Organization (ILO) and the Armenian Young Women's Association (AYWA), the government has established a Start and Develop Your Business Programme, which runs throughout the country. This involves courses in business planning, start-up and mediating business loans. The international review team heard only a brief account of these developments, but wondered how much this training for enterprise incorporated active learning methodologies such as group work, project development, work simulations and mini-enterprise – models of which have already been tested and evaluated elsewhere.

The government also recognises that young people's orientation to the labour market is very low level. Hence the need for a more extensive and comprehensive vocational education and training (VET) system, to prepare young people for the labour market or provide them with appropriate experience. Armenia has been co-operating for five years with both the Swedish Labour Market Board and the Lithuanian Labour Board, and is now acquainted with those systems. The government is working closely with international NGOs (notably the World Bank and the ILO) to produce a co-ordinated approach to understanding and responding to new labour market demands, particularly recognising that Yerevan constitutes a very different economic/labour market context to that found elsewhere in Armenia.

There are many commendable plans, designed to strengthen young people's engagement and attachment to the labour market, in the pipeline. The team heard of a proposed law concerning work experience, to give students the right to a paid or unpaid internship during their studies. They also learned of plans to develop volunteering possibilities that would be counted as important and legitimate experience, though it was not clear quite how this would be achieved. The Department of Social Security spoke of starting to address the predicament of young people who had not completed their general education and had no educational qualifications. The international team was told that this was one of seven groups for whom active labour market measures are being organised: three-month training courses, specialist six-month courses, a small and medium-sized enterprises (SME) business programme and the enhancement of the public works programme that has been in place since 2001.[27]

The most protracted and entrenched labour market problem for Armenia arises, of course, from its relation to neighbouring countries. Conditions militate strongly against effective, successful private sector business enterprise – the communications and social infrastructure is relatively weak, costs are invariably higher and markets are more limited. The advantages for business that often prevail else-

27. The most significant proposal arising out of the National Hearing was that there should be a "tax holiday" for the first two years of employment. The government response was that there could be no such state intervention on this front: "it has to be a completely free market". Members of the international review team challenged this position, maintaining that even the most virulent free market economies still often had dedicated strategies to support young people in finding their first place in the labour market – through training programmes, employment subsidies, recruitment incentives and other measures.

where – taxation, geography, incentives, possibilities for diversification – do not exist in the same way in Armenia. In contrast, everything is likely to be squeezed into a cul-de-sac, from where there is no obvious exit route.

The social, economic and political situation in Armenia makes its challenges around education, training and employment all the more pronounced. Armenia cannot solve these challenges alone, but needs support in creating and improving the conditions in which young people can forge their pathways of transition with more confidence, trust and security.

Education, training and the labour market

Recommendations:

The international review team recognises the immense and complex challenges facing Armenia in "modernising" its approaches to education, training and the labour market. It commends the steps that have already been taken and suggests that key areas that demand sustained focus are:

- the balance between university and vocational education;

- the (lack of) value of much (private non-accredited) university education;

- the possible value in establishing a state non-profit vocational training centre;

- a rebalancing of pedagogical methods, to accommodate less didactic and more active learning, for both personal and enterprise development;

- a stronger emphasis on information and guidance systems relating to career pathways and transitions to the labour market;

- a serious appraisal of the role and function of non-formal education within the "learning pathways" of young people;

- the establishment of enterprise support initiatives such as the kind of micro-credit programmes that have proved successful in other parts of the world (especially in Africa and South America).

---

ii. Health

Young people are typically one of the healthiest groups in most countries, though increasingly they experience disproportionate psycho-social problems arising from their growing dislocation from clear and certain roles within their communities and societies (Rutter and Smith 1993). In Armenia, however, considerably fewer than half of the young people surveyed for the National Report considered themselves to be "completely healthy". The National Report (p. 92) suggests that:

> The destructive earthquake of 1988 that occurred in Armenia, the war in the following years, widespread poverty, unemployment and social polarisation have had their negative effects on youth health.

Such health challenges are exacerbated by the reported evidence that almost three quarters of young people do not participate in physical culture and sports and over half do not trust doctors (National Report, p. 94). Indeed, the National Report (p. 93) suggests that only just over a quarter of young people will consult a doctor for an illness or disease that they do not consider to be life-threatening, with over two thirds preferring to take advice from family members.

Health care, particularly sexual and reproductive health care, was traditionally designed for married women and prospective mothers. For other young people, and especially other young women, there remain significant perceived barriers to accessing medical services (see National Report, p. 97). These may have been formally addressed through recent legislation in Armenia,[28] but it is clear that the perceptions remain. Indeed, the international team was told that explorations of the health and development of young people, made as recently as 2004, revealed that virtually nothing was going on: "there was no policy, no implementation, no data on young people in general and health in particular". Though contraceptives, including condoms, can be purchased in pharmacies, their cost can be prohibitive, according to the health section in the State Youth Policy Strategy – though the National Report (p. 103) survey suggests that the main reason for not using condoms is that they "decrease pleasure". A third of young people surveyed used condoms only occasionally, or not at all.[29]

Health is, however, now a central focus within the State Youth Policy Strategy, in response to growing concerns about reproductive ill-health, sexually transmitted infections and risk behaviours in relation to both legal and illegal substance use (tobacco, alcohol and drugs). There are high levels of unwanted pregnancy and subsequent abortions (many self-induced) among young people.[30]

Practical measures remain, it appears, few and far between. The State Youth Policy Strategy mentions the three new youth health centres that have been established since 1997 (two in Yerevan, one in Vagarshapat). These provide free sexual health education courses, as well as information materials, medical counselling and referrals. UNICEF is supporting the development and implementation of a pilot "healthy lifestyles" education programme in 16 schools, training teachers in its delivery through interactive methods. This started during the academic year 2003-04. UNICEF is also supporting the integration of youth-friendly health services within mainstream health services. There are currently negotiations with the government over the funding of this initiative.

The government, however, did not appear so committed to such "modern" and responsive approaches to health provision for young people. Indeed, the point was made that responsibility for health lay largely with the family (cf. mothers), thus confirming the perspectives of young people surveyed for the National Report. The Ministry of Health also mentioned the UNICEF projects, but said its role was limited to providing approval and a modest financial contribution, although "there may be more involvement in the future". The government, it conceded, did not do much direct work in this area, indicating that it was mainly the domain of NGOs and international organisations.

---

28. The State Youth Policy Strategy reports: "The major achievement in the legal situation is the adoption by the National Parliament of the Republic of Armenia of the Law on 'Reproductive Health and Reproductive Rights of Human Beings' (Law on RH&RR), in December 2002. This Law incorporates internationally recognized Sexual and Reproductive Rights that have been defined in Human Rights terms by the International Planned Parenthood Federation, with special attention to the Rights of Adolescents."

29. This finding obviously upset some of the young people at the National Hearing. They questioned whether these were "objective facts", suggesting that many young Armenians did not have sex at all, so of course they had not used condoms. This is not, however, what the National Report seemed to be suggesting.

30. This proved to be a hotly debated issue during the National Hearing, where it was felt that abortion should be totally condemned and that young women who did not want their babies should still go to full term and then put them up for adoption. One passionate speaker proclaimed that "no Armenian life shall be lost".

It was, indeed, NGOs that appeared to have a much stronger grasp of appropriate responses in policy and practice to the health needs of young people. Between a fifth and a quarter of young people cannot reproduce, because of wider health issues and reproductive tract problems. Many young adults have suffered stress and injury during the conflict with Azerbaijan. The energy crisis of 1993-94, when there was electricity for no more than half an hour a day – and often no food – has taken its toll on the young adult population, who were children at that time. And, though the prevalence of HIV/Aids[31] is arguably not as significant in Armenia compared with some other countries, it is still a source of concern. A national HIV/Aids centre has been established to devise a response. World Vision Armenia also has a dedicated HIV/Aids programme:

> I learned a lot of new information about HIV/Aids from this campaign organized by World Vision and I will share this with my friends and peers because I realized that everybody should be aware of HIV/Aids and try to have some input in the fight against HIV/Aids (Marina, teenage girl from Stepanavan) (World Vision Armenia 2004, p. 15).

It was claimed that there were not, in general, significant problems concerning alcohol use and drug consumption among young people. Smoking, however, is "one of the most dangerous factors influencing health in Armenia, since it is a very widespread and deeply-rooted habit" (National Report, p. 106). The international team was sometimes concerned about the basis upon which such assertions were made and – as with other statistics provided – with the reliability of data. Nonetheless, the international team noted that, despite the huge health challenges of the recent past, there is now the possibility of a relatively healthy diet without the commercial pressures from fast food outlets that have produced major problems concerning childhood and teenage obesity elsewhere. The team did not witness excessive alcohol use.

These points do not mean, however, that health issues are unimportant in Armenia. The National Report (Chapter V) refers to some very significant challenges. Like many other features of youth policy in Armenia, these challenges derive from rapid and dramatic social change as the traditional support, control and guidance mechanisms of family and community lose efficacy, while alternative strategies for providing information, advice and intervention have yet to be developed. Meanwhile, young people are establishing more open lifestyles that are typically characterised by greater risks to health.

Health
Recommendations:

The international team believes that the Government of the Republic of Armenia, through its Ministry of Health, needs to take a much more robust strategic lead in ensuring a strong and coherent response to the youth health challenges in Armenia, especially concerning the sensitive issue of sexual and reproductive health (and the use of condoms as the primary preventative practice to avoid transmitted infections as well as unwanted pregnancy).

The pilot initiative of UNICEF is to be commended and could pave the way for an even more comprehensive personal, health and social education programme of learning within the general education curriculum.

---

31. Very precise detail concerning HIV/Aids and sexually transmitted infections is provided in the State Youth Policy Strategy and in the National Report (pp. 105-106).

There needs to be more attention given to the provision of information concerning both the prevention of health-risk lifestyles and access to health services.

The international team feels that more emphasis should be placed on health checks and other preventative measures.

The critical issue is to develop a framework of health care that allows young people to access it with confidence, when they may feel the need to do so.

iii. Housing

Housing was mentioned as a significant problem for young people, especially students moving to Yerevan and newly married couples, yet the National Report (pp. 39-40) suggests that young people do not believe they have a problem. This is because young people, including young married couples, tend to live with parents. The National Report notes, importantly, that the housing challenge is very different in urban and rural areas. In the latter, housing is not so much of a problem – there are places to live, just no employment and poor communications.

The key issue for Armenia is the changing structure of families, which will produce a very different pattern of demand for housing. The traditional family type (rural, multi-member, many children) is rapidly being replaced by a very different family type – urban, two parents and just one or two children.

The government recognises the new challenges concerning housing and, indeed, the State Insurance Fund is seeking to develop a mortgage lending policy – though whether this will really benefit young people is difficult to tell. There is, nevertheless, a desire to stimulate both private and public sectors in order to establish a more mixed economy of housing provision.

The international team found it difficult to grasp the scale and diversity of the housing issue as it affected young people. It was, nonetheless, made aware that there was a spectrum of issues, ranging from the demand for student accommodation in the capital city to the abject lack of any proper housing for those within the refugee and displaced persons community. Moreover, there seems to be a tension emerging between private (foreign) investment in housing and creating a public response to housing need. This tension is exacerbated by a reported shortage of building materials and workers – meaning that the private and public sectors are in competition with each other, rather than working in a more complementary way. Private demand is driving up prices of materials and labour, making it much harder for NGOs (such as Habitat for Humanity) to sustain their housing plans.

These questions suggest that any response needs to be perhaps unique and certainly creative.

Housing

Recommendations:

The international review team recognises that, although young people themselves do not identify housing as a significant policy challenge, there are major housing dilemmas emerging in Armenia. Creative responses are certainly required. A mortgage market will only respond to one aspect of these dilemmas. There will still be a need for hostels, special housing, rural accommodation and rented housing.

There may be a case for accelerating vocational preparation for skills across the housing sector.

Self-build projects and programmes might be considered.

Shared cost (mortgage and rental) arrangements should be explored.

An overarching housing strategy – developed through consultation between government, NGOs and the private sector (banking and insurance, land investment and property development) – should be produced.

iv. Social protection

Under communism, the issue of social protection did not arise: people had jobs,[32] housing and health care as part of the "social contract". Since independence, with the economic and energy crises, and the war, there were no resources to consider establishing a new system of social protection. Now, however, the international team was told that "measures are being put in place".

For young people, current measures are very limited. There is a meagre unemployment benefit (of US$4 a month) but eligibility is contingent on having been in employment for at least one year.

The international team was not informed of the new measures being proposed and is therefore not in a position to comment on this policy domain, except to note that "safety net" support, even if provided in return for participation in further training or engagement in public works, is a characteristic feature of youth policy throughout much of the rest of Europe.

The international team did not learn enough on the subject of social protection to feel comfortable or confident enough to advance any specific recommendations.

v. Family policy and child welfare

One area in which there has been some attempt at providing social protection has been in relation to families. There has been a point-scoring system for supporting families, which appears to have alleviated the worst of poverty (those living below the poverty line has reduced from 50% to 40% over the past ten years). The World Bank Report (2002) certainly testifies to the value of these benefits when they are paid on time.

The National Report (p. 35) maintains that the family "must be the object of special attention, getting assistance for full implementation of its activities" and, to this end, the government makes an allocation of some 24 million Armenian drams[33] for the social assistance of families. As a result, the birth level, which had dropped dramatically during the 1990s, has marginally increased.

Yet, although family relations are regulated strongly by the constitution (National Report, p. 35) and state youth policy includes all families where a parent is below the age of 30, the family is also a rather private institution. Various NGOs spoke of

---

32. The phenomenon of unemployment only got official recognition in Armenia in 1992 (National Report, p. 27)
33. US$1 = c. 350 drams.

youth policy in Armenia

some of the challenges they faced intervening with families, especially in relation to the promotion of child protection. Their work was often restricted to children who had already been abandoned and were already being looked after in institutional care. World Vision Armenia, for example, has been running a programme since 2004, concerned with the protection of "children in especially difficult circumstances". While this does include children from "vulnerable families", it is still clear that intrusion into family life – even for child protection purposes, and despite many references to the United Nations Convention on the Rights of the Child – is, in terms of traditional Armenian culture, something of a step too far.

> As with social protection, the international team did not feel it learned enough about family policy and child welfare to make any specific proposals or recommendations. Nevertheless, there are clearly models of policies concerning family support and child protection elsewhere that would repay further enquiry and exploration.

vi. Leisure and culture

> In Soviet times, cultural scenarios, lists and the number of presentations were given from above by the government, in the form of instruction, activities of cultural houses and different folk, theatre and other presentations held for youth. Today young people have to look after their cultural requirements themselves, but they don't often succeed (National Report, p. 50).

In 1998, the President of the Republic of Armenia established the Armenian Youth Fund, which is described in the National Report (p. 19) as "the most important arena for solving main youth problems". It has financed and implemented numerous youth events. The president also established, in 2004, the Youth Award of the President of the Republic, which "is granted to talented and gifted young creators in the sphere of fine art and cinema, music and literature".

From the international team's discussions with young people, it appeared that they had little time for "leisure", though many were involved in more traditional cultural pursuits. There remains, in Armenia, a strong focus on traditional culture – contests of piano and violin players every year, puppet shows and annual festivals for national minorities. The Ministry of Sport and Youth Affairs has a culture, leisure and entertainment plan, with specific elements geared towards engaging young people in cultural elements of life: children's literature, cinema and theatre.

In visits to the *marzes*, the international team heard that "although we are in the 21st century we are still a traditional society". Young people were still usually dependent on their families and the bearers of family traditions. Of course, this is also the case in many other parts of Europe: the issue is how tradition and modernity are woven together. Do they clash or complement one another? Young people in rural Armenia might well continue to be the bearers of tradition (for a while at least), but young people in Yerevan are already exposed to a range of global influences.

The State Youth Policy Strategy places great importance on sustaining Armenia's cultural and spiritual heritage and ensuring that young people experience patriotic education (National Report, p. 73). Young people seem able to weave together such traditions and more modern influences. In terms of music, for example, roughly equal proportions prefer Armenian, American and European, and Russian pop music (National Report, p. 81). The National Report (p. 79) notes that young people embrace "both national and universal modern cultural values". Parents involve their children from an early age in singing, music, dancing and sports. By the time they are students, their leisure preferences are music, reading, television and Internet clubs (National Report, p. 63).

The international team was aware that young people do seem to spend most of their time in structured activities of one kind or another (education, work, leisure). Even in Yerevan, there did not appear to be any distinctive youth scenes. Outside Yerevan, young people would have liked access to the cinema or the theatre and to Internet cafes and video games – though most said that their favourite hobby was reading. The international team was conscious of young people looking smart and stylish, but not in the "brand name" fashion and sports styles of western Europe: there are few multinational brands available, even in Yerevan (which is in itself a statement about the economic struggles of Armenia).

There does not seem to be a huge commitment to sports (low levels of physical activity are certainly a concern for health reasons – see above). The international review team asked on a number of occasions what had happened to the former Pioneer and Komsomol buildings, which might have had potential for diversifying leisure opportunities for young people. The response was unclear.[34] Many had been taken over by the private sector, but some were still in use for community purposes, such as leisure and play spaces for children and young people. They are often owned and run by the local community or the Armenian church (see below), though there may also be some state involvement. Some such buildings are not currently in use, but may be developed as part of the regional youth centre strategy that is intended to offer job search support and make other provision for an older age group. Following discussion with the president about state-owned camps, these are going to be given to youth NGOs for management and development. There is, to date, one example of this taking place: a village situated between Yerevan and the international airport had a "culture club" surrounded by casinos. This has now been given to the YMCA for development as youth provision, because parents wanted their children to do something constructive, rather than go to the casinos.

Leisure and culture

Recommendations:

It is a great achievement if the sustaining of traditional cultural attachment can be connected positively to more contemporary leisure interests and pursuits.

The main issue in Armenia concerns the unequal access to a range of both traditional and modern leisure possibilities. Endeavouring to provide a minimum access entitlement for all young people might be a paramount strategic goal, as new provision is developed and old buildings are brought into service to meet the leisure and other needs of children and young people.

---

34. There was some attempt at clarifying this issue during the National Hearing visit, but this was largely to draw attention to the fact that the pan-Armenian Youth Centre is located in a former Komsomol building.

vii. Youth crime and justice

The National Report (p. 108) suggests that just under half of all crimes committed in Armenia in 2003 were perpetrated by young people (under the age of 30): "mainly by men and connected with overusing drugs". It is not untypical for young people to be the main group engaged in offending behaviour – as a general statement – and it is appropriate that the ministry reported paying more attention to youth offending than before. There were intentions to work more closely with the police and to consider issues around crime prevention in particular.

As in all countries, criminal statistics are notoriously unreliable and extremely difficult to interpret. Verbal accounts sometimes clash with published figures. The international team was told that petty crime is "not too bad" amongst young people, but simultaneously the team learned that "petty deviance is commonplace; people break all kinds of rules in Armenia – it is more of a general cultural problem". The State Youth Policy Strategy asserts that the "hard social situation has led to the involvement of a large number of young people in crime aimed at satisfying their needs". Police records suggest that the number of young people aged 14-17 who committed offences in 2004 was 3 051, of whom 432 had previous convictions. Yet the UNICEF country report for 2000 states that the number of registered crimes committed by teenagers was 526,[35] 20% less than the previous year.

The international review team suspects that there is a considerable iceberg of undetected, unreported and unrecorded crime committed by juveniles in Armenia. A police officer observed that many young people are purposefully busy with their education and leisure pursuits and not at all involved in "street life" – "but there are some who don't want to do anything, and if they have no interest in doing anything, they are likely to be interested in crime". In his opinion, youth criminality was increasing and "we need some help in thinking about what to do about it".

The policy response to youth crime is, currently, relatively limited. There is no single age of criminal responsibility – it varies between 14, 16 and 18 for different kinds of offences (National Report, p. 147). Young people under 14 who offend may be placed in special sheltered institutions that are "not prisons, more like orphanages or correctional houses". There is only one youth prison[36] in Armenia, housing some 80[37] young people aged between 14 and 18. This institution was built for much larger numbers in Soviet times, when more young people were imprisoned. Young people held there do receive some rudimentary daily education, including IT (though the International Helsinki Federation for Human Rights report (2005, p. 13) described this curriculum as "fictitious", and also criticised the absence of any kind of psychological support). They care for animals and birds and prepare their own food. Visits are permitted twice a month. According to the staff, the future of the young people there is very contingent on whether or not they get a job on release.

The international team did not learn of any intermediate provision for young people who broke the law. There are no dedicated youth courts, though specialists on juveniles are now present in each court. As the police officer suggested, a serious debate is urgently required.

---

35. If this means recorded crimes it is remarkably low. The pro rata figure for England and Wales would be around 10 000.

36. Abovyan CEI (criminal-executive institution).

37. Again this is strikingly low if contrasted with the 180 or so young offenders aged 10-17 from Wales (population 3 million, like Armenia) who are held in prison or other secure accommodation.

Youth crime and justice

Recommendations:

The prevalence of youth crime does, at least on the surface, appear relatively low. Nevertheless, a more calibrated approach to understanding youth offending (for example, distinguishing between acquisitive and interpersonal crime, or confirming the scale of drug-related crime) would allow for thinking about different kinds of responses.

The government's engagement with the police on this issue is to be welcomed and could perhaps be developed, through bringing in NGOs and perhaps external experts. Community-based responses seem conspicuous by their absence and yet should be the starting point for preventing offending and re-offending, and promoting an approach based on the three platforms of responsibility, restoration and re-integration.

viii. National defence and military service

Time and again, the international team heard that the Armenian army was the largest youth organisation in Armenia, a point emphasised in the National Report (p. 138). Among young people, there is a greater degree of trust in the army than any other government institution. All young men (aged between 18 and 27 years) are required to serve in the army for two years,[38] and there are few exceptions or exemptions (the main ones being having two or more children or remaining as students in postgraduate higher education.[39] And although there has been a law on freedom of conscience and belief since 1991, those who objected to military service for religious reasons were, until 2003, still convicted and imprisoned. The National Report (p. 139) notes that "the controversy of interrelation between military service, religion and beliefs was retained until 2004".

At the end of 2003, however, the Law on Alternative Service was adopted,[40] permitting two alternatives to military service: 36 months alternative military service, carrying no arms, or 42 months work service in the community. The international team was told on a number of occasions that both of these alternatives are regarded as a punishment, yet youth NGOs are reluctant to take a stand against these provisions, in terms of either their content or their duration. Referring to relations with Azerbaijan, one individual commented, "as long as the situation is precarious, we can't do anything". Research suggests that a third of the population has a negative opinion of alternative civilian service (National Report, p. 139) and, despite a wave of criticism from external observers and international bodies about both conditions in military service and alternative service, there appears to be very little

38. *The World Factbook – Armenia* (June 2005) says 12 months.

39. "An important point to mention is that in view of the special attention to enhance the development of science, the constitutions of RA research students have the right to get deferment (delaying the mandatory military service in RA Armed Forces), and afterwards this right maintains its effect if they defend their candidate thesis in due course before the established deadline and start working using their profession" (National Report, p. 68).

40. "[A]n especially lamentable issue was the avoidance or refusal of a number of young people (mainly Jehovah's Witnesses) to serve in RA Armed Forces as a result of which numerous young people were called to justice for deserting.

The law on 'alternative military service' passed in 2003-04 was aimed at addressing the difficult problem of those refusing military service because of their religious beliefs, which enabled a number of young people to serve in RA Armed Forces without going against their beliefs" (National Report, p. 78).

debate inside Armenia.[41] Even the progressive AYLA did not seem to have a defined position on the matter.

The external criticism has focused both on the circumstances of military service and the conditions of alternative service. The European Council of Conscripts Organisations report of 1999 and the International Crisis Group report raised issues such as the compulsory sending of conscripts to Karabakh, when this is meant to be voluntary, and the huge numbers of fatalities during conscript induction rituals. There are also questions about the preparation of young people for life after military service. The International Helsinki Federation for Human Rights (2005, pp. 13-14) advances a range of criticisms relating to alternative service, including its "punitive" duration, the absence of any obligation to inform conscripts of this alternative, and the "unbearable"[42] conditions, in some. There were 49 alternative labour service places available in 2004, but only 20 were applied for: all the applicants were Jehovah's Witnesses.

National defence and military service

Recommendations:

The distinct circumstances of Armenia do, perhaps, make national defence and military service more of a priority within "youth policy" than elsewhere. The international team recognises this fact. So, indeed, do most young people in Armenia, according to survey data which points to *a*. their support and trust in the army and *b*. their general hostility to alternatives to military service.

The few who do elect to take an alternative option have, allegedly, been treated very badly. The international team suggests that a closer look at the structure and content of alternatives to military service would ensure both firmer adherence to human rights and a genuine alternative for the few young people who may wish to consider it. (It is an appalling indictment of this option to read that some participants seek a prison sentence rather than completing it.)

The international team was also concerned about reports of the ill-treatment of conscripts. Attention needs to be given not just to this issue, but also to ways of using time during military service for additional vocational training and other ways of preparing young people for their futures beyond their national service.

The international team believes that youth NGOs should be more assertive in contributing to a debate about the infrastructure, procedures and practices relating both to military and alternative service.

---

41. The issue was a significant focus of comment and discussion at the National Hearing, where the overwhelming view was that any alternative service had to be provided under conditions of "less eligibility", compared to those fulfilling their national duty and serving in the military.

42. Six men performing alternative service in the psychiatric boarding house of the town of Vardenis wanted to terminate their service and serve a prison sentence instead. Their parents told the International Helsinki Federation for Human Rights that they had to work with seriously ill people, wash them and their laundry. They were forbidden to leave the territory of the hospital and they were accommodated in one room and had no possibility to shower. They had to work from 7 a.m. to 9 p.m. and eat the same food as the patients, which was sub-standard. Military police checked on them several times a week and threatened them with charges for not carrying out military service. The director of the hospital told the parents that he only carried out orders "coming from above", which advised him to create unbearable conditions for those performing alternative service (International Helsinki Federation for Human Rights 2005, p. 14).

ix. Values and religion

Young people believe that the Armenian Apostolic Church should be involved in promulgating actively national and universal Christian values: "in this respect, the importance of the Armenian Apostolic Church clergy operating in the RA National Armed Forces is highlighted as an important factor in developing military and patriotic spirit in young soldiers" (National Report, p. 76). Indeed, the vast majority of the Armenian population (94%, according to *The World Factbook*) are members of the Armenian Apostolic Church: "being a national Christian Church, it manages to become the main uniting force for the Armenian nation and the satisfier of the latter's spiritual needs in social life" (National Report, p. 75). The history of the Armenian Apostolic Church is a mandatory subject within the general educational curriculum, and the National Report (p. 75) maintains that the church now has still greater prominence in the lives of young people than even a decade ago. It is also argued that it helps the Armenian diaspora "to preserve national identity and national education" (National Report, p. 76). In contrast, however, the National Report (p. 88) also deplores the subordination of spiritual values to more material and "surface value" concerns:

> As a result of this, most of youth adheres to an insufficient value system and prioritises irresponsibility towards state and society, idolises material values and neglects civic obligations.

Once more, as with the debate around leisure and culture, one sees a creative tension, conflict and possible reconciliation between tradition and modernity.[43] It is quite clear that many young people in Armenia are being exposed, more and more, to other values: Western values, democratic values, European values. The question (also addressed in the National Report, p. 85) is how these are being absorbed and made sense of within the Armenian context, culture and history – a tradition of patriotic education, Christian morality and humanism. There is huge pride in Armenia as the "first Christian country". The Armenian Apostolic Church is inseparable from Armenia's national identity. The church continues to provide both spiritual and more pragmatic support for the majority of young people.

Nevertheless, there are small minorities of people who do not subscribe to this church, and follow new religious movements. The National Report (p. 74) describes those religious organisations currently registered in Armenia, and discusses those which are not (National Report, p. 77). Concern was expressed to the international team about the increasing affiliation of young people to "dangerous" sects that were active in exploiting the uncertainties being experienced by young people in difficult times.

Values and religion

Recommendations:

Armenia has formal legislation concerned with liberty of conscience and freedom in the expression of religious beliefs. The International Helsinki Federation for Human Rights (2005, p. 13) – following some criticism of a

---

43. A recurrent preoccupation during the National Hearing was how "traditional Armenian values" were to be protected against the intrusion of alternative values arising from globalisation and "European integration".

registration in 2004 – reports that a new law on religious activities is being drafted.

For the vast majority of the population, there is daily affirmation – through the activities of both the Armenian Apostolic Church and the state – of a framework of values that inform the national identity. Over the last decade, this has proved supportive for the majority of young people.

The international team is aware, however, of encroachment on this mainstream position from two sources: *a.* more modern, alternative/additional values deriving from non-Armenian and democratic contexts; *b.* competing religious organisations, both official (i.e. those registered) and those designated as "sects" in Armenia.

The international team recognises concerns about the potentially negative influence of both of these. It also acknowledges the desire on the part of many people in Armenia, including the government, to preserve and sustain traditional values. It recommends, however, that the way to address these issues is through information and discussion, so that young people can make informed choices.

Chapter 5: Themes — key issues for youth policy

Participation and citizenship

The year in which the international review of youth policy in Armenia was conducted was also the European Year of Citizenship through Education. Apparently, Armenia set up a National Committee to co-ordinate activities on this front (the theme for March 2005, for example, was "education for the participation of young people in local and regional life") but the international review team heard no direct references to this programme of events.[44]

Nevertheless, youth participation was described by the Deputy Minister for Youth Affairs as "the most important problem in the country". She suggested that when young people did get involved, they could address many of the wider challenges facing them in Armenia, "but young people don't get involved enough". Certainly, in terms of political participation, the National Report survey (p. 124) indicates that "only 3.6% are members of some political party and 5% have confidence in a political party". Armenian youth, as a rule, "does not show active participation either in local governmental or nationwide election processes" – they are indifferent, think their vote will make no difference, and don't trust the justice and transparency of elections. Only 30 of the 80 political parties in Armenia have youth wings and only five MPs (just two with a party affiliation) under the age of 30 were elected in the parliamentary elections of 2003 (National Report, p. 123).

This refers, of course, to political participation and the United Nations World Programme of Action for Youth defines youth involvement across four dimensions, which are repeated in Armenia's State Youth Policy Strategy:

- economic participation (work and entrepreneurship);
- political participation (decision-making and the assignment of authority);
- social participation (involvement in public and community life);
- cultural participation (self-realisation and creative self-expression).

The National Report (p. 111) maintains that:

---

44. The Armenian authorities indicated that, in accordance with the State Youth Policy Strategy for 2006-07, the Ministry of Foreign Affairs and the Ministry of Culture and Youth Affairs will come up with an initiative to join the European Charter on the Participation of Young People in Local and Regional Life.

The institutions dealing with the issue of participation are political parties, NGOs, trade unions, student unions and other youth associations, as well as mass media which are the main instruments ensuring youth participation ....

The issue of youth civic participation is one of the critical problems in the frameworks of governmental policy on youth affairs.

The State Youth Policy Strategy suggests that there have been slow improvements in the development of youth participation and civil society, but this is "not sufficiently developed". There is passivity around political engagement and inadequate engagement of youth NGOs in the formulation of youth policy. In addition, there are funding problems around building volunteering and youth organisations, and poor provision of culture and sports institutions (particularly in rural areas) inhibiting possibilities for self-development.

The State Youth Policy Strategy provides statistical and other information about the progress of youth participation in Armenia – this does not need repeating here. Suffice it to say that, since the appointment of a Deputy Minister for Youth Affairs and a discrete state budget for the youth sector (since 1998), there have been significant steps forward, although there is still a serious deficit of trust in both government and NGOs.

Civic and political participation is a substantial item in the National Report (Chapter VI) but, despite everything that it says, there are issues that are not covered. Though everyone who is born in the Republic of Armenia has formal citizenship, there are key questions about the capacity of certain sub-sections of the youth population to participate: young people in remote rural areas, refugees and internally displaced persons, as well as those who come from small minority ethnic groups. Those who do secure possibilities for participation – through, for example, privileged positions within favoured youth organisations, or through governance of universities – are arguably a very small, and elite, minority. Of course, the legacy of communism is a lack of trust in institutional, organised life and it will take time to strengthen mechanisms and structures for participation and an active sense of citizenship. The entrenched dependency culture – waiting for something to happen – clearly also has to be addressed. And, for many young people, their need to survive socially, educationally and economically is likely to reduce both their capacity and motivation for active participation.

In Armenia, it seems, participation is integrally linked to the issue of information (see below). Greater transparency, trust and institutional reliability are fundamental pre-requisites to fostering a greater commitment to participation in civic and political life. Many people who spoke to the international team felt that they were not properly informed and that all relevant and important information was kept close to a few favoured youth NGOs that themselves sought to protect their own privileged position.

Participation and citizenship

Recommendations:

The international team believes that serious attention needs to be paid to the revised European Charter on the Participation of Young People in Local and Regional Life, ensuring youth organisations are fully engaged in debate on governmental policy matters that may affect young people, ensuring a critical dialogue with youth NGOs, and promoting the value of such processes through media communication, thereby building trust and encour-

> aging more young people to become involved. This might be best advanced under the patronage of the president.

Combating social exclusion and promoting inclusion

The National Report identifies two particularly vulnerable groups of young people in Armenia: those with disabilities and refugees. The challenges that face them are, in many respects, simply accentuated versions of those that face most young people – such as education, employment, housing, social and cultural opportunities. In other respects, however, their challenges are distinct and unique and require a dedicated policy response if their greater social inclusion is to be secured. There is also a dramatic urban/rural divide that demands attention.

There are around 130 000 people with disabilities, including not only those with disabilities through birth and accident, but significant numbers disabled through the earthquake and the war. These include considerable numbers of young people. One might have thought that this would have produced a more accepting attitude towards people with disabilities but, according to the main disability NGO, PYUNIC,[45] there is still limited acceptance and little acknowledgement of their distinctive support needs.

During the 1990s, Armenia received almost 400 000 refugees, primarily as a result of the war with Azerbaijan and the conflict over Nagorno-Karabakh (National Report, p. 53). Some initially hoped to return; others wanted to stay. When it became clear that none would be able to return, the government established a refugee integration policy. Besides typical problems faced by all excluded groups, refugees often came from urban areas and struggled to adjust to rural living. Many also spoke Russian, rather than Armenian. YMCA Armenia has been one of the more active NGOs in working with refugee children and young people, focusing on ten villages and organising a summer camp for each one, where children aged 12-14 are trained in computers, and participate in games and other (non-formal[46]) learning activities. It is hoped that these children and young people will take the ideas and methods back to their villages and disseminate them. However, one continuing concern is that refugee young people are unable to participate in youth development programmes outside Armenia, a position about which the Deputy Minister for Youth Affairs has persistently sought some kind of resolution.

One third of the population of Armenia live in rural areas. It is from those areas that many young people emigrate both to the cities and to other countries (see below). Many young people go to Yerevan to study and then never return to their native regions. Many take seasonal work in Russia and other countries and return home in between. There is very little employment in the villages, though officially there is very little unemployment either, because most people are attached to land. There

---

45. PYUNIC, the Armenian Association for the Disabled, receives much of its funding through the Armenian diaspora, especially from the United States. It campaigns for disability rights and makes direct provision for people with disabilities. For example, it provides some 200 wheelchairs, while the government provides 500. PYUNIC appears to have strong and positive relations with government departments and believes that it has helped to change attitudes around disabilities for the better, particularly since the earthquake and the war.

46. The Director of YMCA Armenia spoke of carrying out some human rights and democracy education, through games, using training programmes and methodologies from European partner organisations, and also materials such as the T-kits of the Council of Europe Directorate of Youth and Sport.

is also very little opportunity for community participation and social life, which is usually only available in more urban and populated areas.

By broader European standards, a very large proportion of young people in Armenia would be considered as "excluded", though perhaps many are not thought of as such within Armenian norms and according to their reference points. Most young people still benefit, for example, from the support of their families. There are, therefore, different conceptions of exclusion and these generate different ideas about inclusion. There is clearly, however, a need for dedicated attention to the specific needs of groups of particular young people. Though market forces may slowly improve the position of many young people, they cannot be relied upon to improve the lot of these excluded groups.

Combating exclusion and promoting inclusion

Recommendations:

At least three distinctive groups of young people are more clearly socially excluded than others, even in the difficult and challenging social and economic context of Armenia. These are young people with disabilities, refugees and those who live in remote rural areas.

The international team heard repeatedly that the hope of social inclusion rested on improvements in the market economy. This is not a realistic proposition or belief. The "market" cannot be seen as a value system and left to itself – this will inevitably produce even greater social polarisation. There has to be action and activity beyond the market: democracy, individuality, civil society, state intervention. A balanced social market economy has to be the aspiration, not unfettered capitalism, which will compound the exclusion of many. To promote social inclusion, there need to be strategies that are enabling, restricting and regulating – regional development plans that consider the needs of young people, especially those who are most marginalised. The whole concept of civil society is based on values that mediate and interplay between the public administration and the market. The market has to operate within a set of rules established by the state. The market is beyond trade.

The international team felt that Armenia needs to convene a high level debate that may help to demystify the "market" as some kind of sacred entity, and support the development of a strategy that may address the worst excesses of exclusion currently being experienced by some groups of young people.

Youth information

One of the main alternatives to a didactic approach to learning is for young people to "download", digest and distil information for themselves. It is now a truism to speak of living in the "information age" and the "knowledge society", but there are now numerous sources of information available beyond the family, school and church – through the mass media. The National Report (p. 126) acknowledges this fact:

> The provision of a decent life for a young man (*sic*) is impossible without the accessibility of information and communication. This is the main reason for top-listing information

among European and international standards of youth national report assessment. This chapter (6.3) of the report is dedicated to that issue.

There are three issues here: the provision of information, the capacity of young people to access it and the skills of young people to make constructive use of it. In Armenia there are significant obstacles at all three stages (National Report, p. 134). While in many countries the Internet is now almost taken for granted, over half of young people in Armenia say they do not have access to it (National Report, p. 64), and television remains the most widespread information source (National Report, p. 68). The international team also heard, from both experts and young people, that boys tended to make far greater use of the Internet. Even where girls had access to the Internet (through their schools, for example) they appeared not to be actively encouraged to learn how to make best use of it.

There are piecemeal efforts to improve the provision of information to young people. The Ministry of Sport and Youth Affairs has published a youth newspaper since 2004 and the ministry has, since 2005, also operated its own website: www.youth-policy.am (National Report, p. 18). At the start of 2006, there was the intention of broadcasting a youth television programme twice a month:

> which will represent youth needs, tasks and expectations, will elucidate those youth public events, which are missed from main press, it will acquaint the passive part of youth with NGO's life and assist the process of integration in international public life (National Report, p. 18).

The Armanian Young Lawyers Association (AYLA) has published and distributed leaflets to raise awareness amongst young people of their legal rights (see National Report, p. 143). The planned youth centres in the regions (see above) will also support the dissemination of information of relevance and interest to young people, particularly as they will allow access to the Internet.

Youth information

Recommendations:

There have been some questions raised about the objectivity and impartiality of the media in Armenia (see International Helsinki Federation for Human Rights 2005, pp. 4-6. This notwithstanding, the international team welcomes the commitment by the Ministry of Sport and Youth Affairs to improve the volume and quality of youth information provision.

The international team believes that Armenia needs to consider reinforcing youth information strategy, possibly through the offices of a youth information agency. There are models and concepts of youth information services – covering issues such as the ethics of youth information provision and the human support required.

Youth information is very closely connected to wider advice and guidance services, which are clearly required by young people in relation to employment, vocational direction, educational studies, mobility options, ICT training, health issues and business and enterprise development, for example.

Regional youth centres, which are ideal "satellites" for the delivery of a structured youth information service, are being set up, as well as training to ensure that information is appropriately channelled and young people are properly supported as they endeavour to make sense of it and act upon it.

> Only if it is done in this way will such provision be perceived as transparent, reliable and trustworthy.

Multiculturalism and minorities

Armenia is a strongly homogeneous society. Though the Armenian diaspora constitutes a minority in many other parts of the world, in Armenia itself there is almost no concept of a minority. *The World Factbook* (2005, using data from 2002) reports that the ethnic composition of Armenia is 93% Armenian, less than 1% Azeri ("as at the end of 1993, virtually all Azeris had emigrated from Armenia"), 2% Russian and 4% other,[47] mostly Yezedi.[48] The latter "have been living with the Armenian people, side by side, since remote times" (National Report, p. 82), but recently their population has declined because of emigration.

Thus, within Armenia, there is little point in speaking of multiculturalism[49] and such talk, coupled with considerations of intercultural learning, relate more to potential new horizons for the region in the future.

Mobility and internationalism

The new horizons that are sometimes anticipated for Armenia and Armenians are unlikely to be achieved until a range of obstacles has been overcome. In relation to Azerbaijan and Turkey, these are long-standing political issues beyond the remit of this report, but they do obstruct the possibilities for engagement by young people in Armenia within the wider international context of youth development. Of course, many young Armenians secure their own personal development through mobility, supported in both material and emotional ways by relatives among the Armenian diaspora. Other young Armenians, regrettably, experience "internationalism" through the increasing prevalence of trafficking, particularly of young women.

Many Armenians (some estimates suggest approaching one million people) have left Armenia for good since 1991, because of the serious social and economic problems. Young people constitute about 20% of these – possibly, therefore, up to 200 000 individuals – with significant consequences for marriage and family formation, as well as broader demographics. Armenia, for other reasons as well, has a low fertility rate (1.32 children per woman) and therefore an ageing population. It has been referred to as a "cemetery country". Yet, paradoxically, the long history of emigration from Armenia has contributed to its survival, for it has relied upon remittances from abroad, not just for supporting families but for economic renewal and development (investment and business enterprise). It is estimated that over US$1 billion enters the Armenian economy in this way each year.

Many more Armenians work abroad, particularly in current CIS and former Soviet countries such as Georgia, Belarus and Ukraine. The question of tax and social

---

47. See National Report, p. 82.

48. See *The World Factbook* for more information about minorities in Armenia: https://www.cia.gov/cia/publications/factbook/geos/am.html.

49. There is arguably, however, an urgent case for talking about the place of minorities in Armenian society. This was not an issue that was raised during the international visits, but it was advanced during the National Hearing, when a young person from the Polish minority asked the "international experts" how such minorities were perceived and treated in other countries and what was being done in those places to stem the tide of emigration. Illustrations of different approaches – in Norway, Cyprus, and South Korea – were given in response.

insurance payments in those countries – and whether there should be remittances for Armenia to support future unemployment and pension payments to individuals who have worked there – is a continual issue for negotiation. Young Armenians also often say that, if they had the chance, they would leave the country as emigrants or migrants (mainly as a result of social and economic problems) in order to provide for their families and improve their living conditions. However, more severe border and visa restrictions and requirements have limited the possibilities of doing so legitimately, which has led to a sharp increase in illegal migration and the illegal transportation of migrants. This has taken place in parallel to the illegal trafficking of people, notably young women (National Report, pp. 148-150).

The issue of migration (both legal and illicit) and trafficking is also a major focus of the State Youth Policy Strategy. Even prior to the acceptance of the youth strategy, the government of Armenia had taken legislative steps to comply with international standards in establishing the prevalence of trafficking, carrying out preventative activities, as well as providing support and assistance to those affected.

The international team received competing perspectives about the issue of internal migration within Armenia. The National Report (p. 44) suggested that around 10% of young people have changed their place of residence in the past five years. Some young people disputed that there was an automatic tendency for internal migration from the countryside to the cities; there was now some value in staying in the country. Though they may earn little money, there was the important support of the family and a growing commitment by the state to support regional development through regional youth centres, training programmes for the young unemployed (in traditional rural skills) and business support. Provision of cultural festivals and activities and increasing access to the Internet were also growing. Some student organisations and regional NGOs reported that the situation was no longer as bleak in the countryside, and that the pace of out-migration by young people was slowing down. There was now perhaps more optimism about the future than had existed just a few years ago.

Beyond work and studying abroad, there is the issue of Armenia's connection with broader international (notably European) youth development activities, especially as Armenia is now a participant in the European Neighbourhood Policy of the European Union 2006-13. The Deputy Minister for Youth Affairs has been a very active participant in the work of the Council of Europe Directorate of Youth and Sport over the past few years. The European Voluntary Service (EVS) element of the EU Youth Programme (soon to be Youth in Action) now has a co-operation agreement with the Caucasus. All these developments suggest that there is space for development for young people in Armenia, with relation to constructive mobility and international links.

Mobility and internationalism

Recommendations:

The international team believes that Armenian youth policy may benefit significantly from engaging more closely with the EU Youth in Action programme and the European Neighbourhood Policy. The EU and the Council of Europe Directorate of Youth and Sport can serve as a bridge, combating the isolation of Armenia and opening up its intellectual and conceptual, if not (yet) its political and geographical, borders.

> The international team feels that Armenia should seek closer collaboration with the practical measures of the EU Youth in Action programme, which are already established in relation to the European Voluntary Service (EVS).
>
> The Armenian diaspora may wish to consider mechanisms for supporting more communication, contacts and exchanges between Armenian young people and their counterparts in the wider Europe.

Equal opportunities

> The State Youth Policy of RA must encompass a sufficient number of resources, alongside already existing entities, in order to implement an effective policy aiming at the provision of equal rights and opportunities for both men and women at the level of the younger generation (National Report, p. 133).

In 2004 the Armenian Government approved the 2004-10 national Action Plan on the Improvement of Women's Situation and the Enhancement of their Role in Society:

> The programme aims at meeting commitments and obligations defined by international documents and will foster provision of equal opportunities and equal rights for both men and women as a prerequisite for shaping a democratic and legal state and establishing a civic society (National Report, p. 130).

Formal communication with the international team constantly emphasised the commitment in Armenia to equal opportunities. The National Report (p. 131) mentions that "the traditions of equal involvement in elementary education go back to the 19th century". It goes on, however, to indicate that a disproportionate number of men continue their studies to doctoral level.

The international team heard of a special gender project with eight different lines concerning different issues in employment and addressing seven different "vulnerable" sub-groups of women. The international team also heard of equal access to education for people with disabilities, and that all organisational services were open to everyone, irrespective of religion, sexuality or ethnic group.

The day-to-day reality conveyed to the international team was, however, very different. Irrespective of qualifications, there was still a strong expectation that women would leave the labour market and produce a family. The international team heard deep concerns expressed about trafficking women. Conversely, there was little discussion on the subject of domestic violence. The team also did not hear any discussion of the rights of gay men and women, despite awareness of the damning indictment of Armenia's treatment of homosexuals in a report by the International Helsinki Federation for Human Rights[50] (2005). Although the disability NGO, PYUNIC, maintained that the state accepted the right of disabled people to social protection, the international team heard about widespread discrimination against people with disabilities in social and economic life.

As a result of this dissonance between official rhetoric and "regulation" and reported reality, the international team concluded that Armenia remains some way distant from where it could or should be in relation to European standards and

---

50. "Armenian legislation does not contain a single provision on discrimination based on or due to sexual orientation" (International Helsinki Federation for Human Rights 2005, p. 14).

practices. There are, of course, always elements of such dissonance in most countries, but the gulf to be bridged in Armenia appears to be considerable.

Equal opportunities

Recommendations:

Most countries now formally express their commitment to equal opportunities by stating that people will not be discriminated against on the grounds of gender, race, disability, religious persuasion or sexual orientation. According to the Armenian Constitution, all forms of discrimination are prohibited.

The international team had little direct contact with anyone who might conceivably have had direct experience of unequal opportunities. Indeed, its meetings were almost exclusively with senior professionals who were clearly part of a privileged elite.

Evidence of discriminatory practices were, however, received secondhand through verbal reports or written documentation. This information was, nevertheless, sufficient for the international team to have concerns about the prospects in Armenian society for young people who did not conform to mainstream, dominant characteristics in that society.[51]

---

51. Owing to considerable delay, for various reasons, in the scheduling of an international hearing for the Armenia youth policy review before the statutory bodies of the youth sector of the Council of Europe, it is important to register here two reports that have appeared since the production of the international review team's international report in mid-June 2006. First, there was the report of the European Commission against Racism and Intolerance (ECRI) on Armenia (30 June 2006). Second, there was the report by the Council of Europe Commissioner for Human Rights following his visit to Armenia on 7-11 October 2007. Both reports highlighted progress made in areas such as equality, women's rights and the situation of minorities.

Chapter 6: Supporting youth policy

The idea of youth policy remains a relatively new concept in Armenia (it is relatively new everywhere), but there is already a significant core of advocates for more coherence and development. This includes the material and strategic support of the diaspora, through the pan-Armenian International Youth Centre Foundation and the All-Armenian Fund.[52] It counts among its political supporters both the president and the prime minister, and more specifically the office of the Deputy Minister for Youth Affairs (Ms Lilit Asatryan, at the time of the review) who had acquired a reputation across Europe for dynamic engagement with the youth policy agenda. There is no reason to suppose that her successor as deputy minister, Mr Arthur Poghsyan, will not sustain the momentum for youth policy development in Armenia. Beyond the government, there are the international donor organisations which often have a specific interest in the needs of children and young people, and the general NGOs and specific youth NGOs within Armenia that are endeavouring to develop specific services for young people. The youth NGOs receiving government support (through the Centre for Organising Events) are perceived by some to be over-deferential to the political administration, but they are nevertheless active in supporting youth policy at the levels of both policy and practice. The point here is not to discuss the wider infrastructure that might play more of a part in Armenia's youth policy (which, no doubt, would be a good thing), but to identify the key players and structures that are already doing so. This is, in the view of the international team, a very useful foundation on which to build.

There are, however, professional (rather than political) cornerstones, which help to sustain youth policy development: youth research, training and mechanisms for the dissemination of good practice.

Youth research

A page towards the beginning of the National Report (p. 22) is dedicated to emphasising the importance of having a research dimension to youth policy formulation and development. Nevertheless, the international team was told that, for many reasons, research-based understanding of young people in Armenia tends to be rather fragmented and sometimes of questionable reliability.

There are a number of significant reports, but these have often been produced for international donor organisations or for specific purposes. The international team heard that "researchers are not very objective", suggesting that too often reports were prepared to suit an agenda that was already in progress. "The numbers may

---

52. The Armenian authorities underlined that there are no finances allocated from the diaspora through these above-mentioned funds for youth policy implementation.

get twisted", it was suggested, in order to secure further funding for particular pieces of work.

Nevertheless, the view was that independent and more reliable youth researchers were gradually emerging, including those who were charged with producing the National Report. There was, however, a feeling that, even if youth research findings had increasing credibility, they would not necessarily influence the policy debate, unless they were championed by members of the political elite. In some respects, this is not surprising (it is the case everywhere, to some extent), but the message was that the fragments of youth research that do exist ("nothing comprehensive, but it all contributes", one individual said) are rather disconnected from the youth policy-making agenda and debate.

Youth research

Recommendations:

Whatever the deficiencies of their focus and findings, there were 5 000 Russian youth researchers in Soviet times. The international team passed a door in Yerevan saying "HAUK – Youth-Public Analytical Centre", but surprisingly never heard from them.

Studies of themes and issues concerning young people (such as HIV/Aids) appear to be segmented, often prepared in isolation in response to the needs and demands of international NGO priorities and activities.

The international team believes that there needs to be a negotiated but more systematic approach to youth studies, with – in time – a dedicated group of people studying the lifestyles and transitions of young people in Armenia. There is clearly a need for a sociology of youth – the model that exists in Slovenia would be worthy of exploration.

Training

The main training that has been carried out in Armenia on youth issues seems to have been done by a small group of individuals whose experience is through European networks (the Council of Europe, and the SALTO centres[53]). There is now a trainers' pool in Armenia, and at least one Armenian youth trainer is a member of the Council of Europe's trainers' pool.

Once again, this is a foundation on which to build, but the next step is to consider the balance, range and content of training practice. However limited it may be, there is a risk that it will remain over-functional (focused on "how to" – methodology) rather than more thematic (focused on "what to" – key issues and objectives). There is also a risk that training practice ends up hiding within its own process – doing training for its own sake or because it is a way of securing financial support. Finally, there were concerns expressed by the international team that newsletters and websites become the sole mechanism for distributing information and ideas. This can create an unhealthy dependency on these components, at the expense of others, such as the YMCA summer camp for children in the villages – which has much more chance of producing enterprise and leadership, as well as a multiplier effect on the children's contemporaries who did not take part.

---

53. SALTO stands for Support, Advanced Learning and Training Opportunities. The SALTO centres are resource centres working on European priority areas within the youth field.

The dissemination of good practice

The international team witnessed or heard of many islands of good practice – the disability projects of PYUNIC, World Vision's child assessment plan, the work of the Armenian Young Lawyers' Association (AYLA) and the regional training by the YMCA. The question that always has to be asked is the extent to which knowledge about such programmes (their design, costs, methodologies, impact) is disseminated and discussed in a broader context. Can they be replicated and multiplied? What have been the main challenges and weaknesses around their delivery?

Too often, the team felt, programmes and projects take place in a climate of competition and therefore some secrecy. Glossy brochures telling of unhindered success (without going into too much detail!) are the order of the day. There is a reticence about admitting difficulties or sharing the bases of success. Where ideas are pulled together and shared, this seems to be a product of accidental contact, rather than a structured and systematic organisation. The international team heard very little about quality standards, external scrutiny or purposeful evaluation.

In June 2005, the very first NGO market ever took place in Armenia, where NGOs literally "set out their stalls". This was an important stepping stone in improving transparency in the work of NGOs and broadcasting what they believe they are doing best. It is perhaps a model to be replicated in the regions, possibly through the new regional youth centres that are being established.

Chapter 6: Supporting youth policy

Chapter 7: Conclusion

One individual the team spoke to summarised a host of issues that were repeatedly expressed to the international team:

> The Soviet Union collapsed and the huge industries were privatised. People couldn't run these industries (because of supply chain problems) and things were made worse by the war and the ensuing blockade. Even when we do make a surplus there is no market, we can't sell because of the blockade.

> The people who run this country grew up in Soviet times and are still trapped in that mind-set. That is the problem. I think that young people are becoming more innovative and self-directing and ready for progress. Young people in Armenia are looking towards Europe with optimism, but things remain hard for them.

> We need to think about our country in the 1920s. After the Ottoman Empire, Armenia joined the Soviet Union – we had an economy, industry and health. Armenia was a leader in the Soviet Union. Maybe it killed personal initiative, but young people with education knew they could get a job.

There is a mind-set and a collective memory – a history – in Armenia that must be taken seriously and cannot be overlooked. But there is also a contemporary context – a modernity – in which young people express frustration about being unable to realise their aspirations and potential, significantly because they cannot live in harmony with their neighbours.

At another meeting, the point was made to the international team that "we need to think hard about what kind of young people we want to have in Armenia and therefore should be considering what we should be doing for the children – because they will be the youth of the future". This may seem almost a platitude, but it implicitly captures a tension that was witnessed repeatedly by the international team. Is youth policy about producing soldiers and mothers who can protect and sustain the identity and integrity of the Armenian nation? Or is youth policy about preparing young people who have enterprise and initiative so that they can play an equal and active part, both economically and through civil society, in an enlarging Europe?

This is a tension in youth policy, but it is a tension derived from the profound pressures and challenges facing Armenia – between past and present, East and West, traditional and modern values, passivity and activity, acceptance and argument. There is also an Armenian context of official politics and policies and an Armenian world of young people, with their specific dreams and aspirations. The key word that threads through all these dilemmas and tensions is "reconciliation", and the key question is how might this be achieved? The international team heard from an individual speaking on the subject of establishing civil society and engaging with the wider Europe:

> It is always a question of values and ideas. In a globalising world, we need to find our place as Armenians – to keep our culture and identity. I can't say if we are an open or closed society, but I know we need to have a dialogue about values. Democracy can be developed in any country, but to establish civil society takes time. There is a problem of voluntary engagement by young people in the work of NGOs. Education is the critical thing – it affects everything. We have to think about what kind of education to provide, the liberal and democratic values to provide, so the youth can build the country. But we must not forget where we have come from and who we are.

> I think the market makes itself, but not completely on its own. The market is also affected by the ideas that prevail in any society, and by the political and geographical conditions. We are still struggling to find the right path.

The path for young people in Armenia has, until very recently (and one must not forget the recency of "modern" developments) been clearly mapped, guided and governed by family, school and state. It is now less clear, less certain and more risky – particularly for young people struggling to secure the basic essentials of life. For those young people, speaking of "spaces for creativity" and engaging in "non-formal" learning probably has something of a hollow ring. Both personal identity and prospective futures have become less fixed and more precarious. No wonder the National Report suggests that many young Armenians remain deeply anxious about their futures.

There are, nonetheless, youth policy initiatives that must be attempted and developed: the promotion of participation, the provision of information, the securing of trust in official procedures and institutions, the encouragement of enterprise and healthy lifestyles and effecting change in the structure and content of the general education curriculum. There are perhaps also other more "private" issues (such as sexuality and possibly disability), which are not yet acknowledged as "public" issues, which should be legitimate components of youth policy.

Even though Armenia has now endorsed its State Youth Policy Strategy, the debate on youth policy is in many ways just starting. It is a debate that needs to be taken beyond a political and professional inner circle, though this has driven policy and practice so far. It is a debate that needs to pull together the many strands of existing youth policy – which are currently being delivered by a disparate group of players – and to knock them into a more coherent and structured form, realisable with the resources that are currently or prospectively available. And it is a debate that needs to establish the desired balance and interaction between an affirmative position, characteristic of traditional Armenia, and an anticipatory position relating to Armenia's aspirations for the future.

References and other texts consulted

Armenian Young Lawyers Association (2003), *2004-2006 Strategic Plan of Armenian Young Lawyers Association*, Yerevan: Armenian Young Lawyers Association

Armenian Young Lawyers Association (2004), *2003 Annual Report*, Yerevan: Armenian Young Lawyers Association

Denstad, F. and Flessenkemper, T. (2004), *Mission Report: Development of a youth strategy in Armenia*, Yerevan: UNICEF Armenia

European Commission (2001), *A new impetus for European youth: White Paper*, Brussels: European Commission

Government of the Republic of Armenia (1998), *Conception of State Youth Policy: Adopted by the Government of Republic of Armenia*, Yerevan: Ministry of Sport and Youth Affairs of the Republic of Armenia

Government of the Republic of Armenia (2004), *Youth Policy Strategy (draft)*, Yerevan: Ministry of Sport and Youth Affairs of the Republic of Armenia

Government of the Republic of Armenia (2005), *State Youth Policy Strategy for 2005-2007* (draft), Yerevan: Ministry of Sport and Youth Affairs of the Republic of Armenia

Hovannisian, R. (2004), "The Republic of Armenia", in R. Hovannisian (ed.), *Armenian People from Ancient to Modern Times: Vol. II Foreign Dominion to Statehood – The Fifteenth Century to the Twentieth Century*, London: Palgrave Macmillan

International Helsinki Federation for Human Rights (2005), *Human Rights in the OSCE Region: Europe, Central Asia and North America, Report 2005 (Events of 2004): Armenia*, Vienna: International Helsinki Federation for Human Rights

Markosyan, R., Tadevosyan, A. and Sinanyan, A. (2002), *Youth Policy, International Co-operation and Conflict Resolution: Educational Report of the Training Course*, Yerevan: Network of Armenian Youth Organisations

Ministry of Sport and Youth Affairs (2008), *National Youth Report of Armenia*, Yerevan: Youth Policy Department, ISBN 978-99941-2-6145-8

Parliamentary Assembly of the Council of Europe (2004a), *Resolution 1361: Honouring of obligations and commitments by Armenia*, Doc. 10027, report of the Committee on the Honouring of Obligations and Commitments by Member States of the Council of Europe (Monitoring Committee). Text adopted by the Assembly on 27 January 2004.

Parliamentary Assembly of the Council of Europe (2004b), *Implementation of Resolutions 1361 (2004) and 1374 (2004) on the honouring of obligations and commitments by Armenia*, Doc. 10286, report of the Committee on the Honouring of Obligations and Commitments by Member States of the Council of Europe (Monitoring Committee). Text adopted by the Assembly on 15 September 2004.

PYUNIC: Armenian Association for the Disabled (2000), *Highlights: Summary of Activities 2000*, Van Nuys, California: PYUNIC

PYUNIC: Armenian Association for the Disabled (2003), *Highlights: Summary of Activities 2003*, Van Nuys, California: PYUNIC

PYUNIC: Armenian Association for the Disabled (2005), *History of the Armenian Association for the Disabled "PYUNIC"*, Yerevan: PYUNIC

Rutter, M. and Smith, D. (eds) (1993), *Psycho-social disorders in young people: time trends and their causes*, London: Heinemann

The World Factbook: Armenia, www.cia.gov/publications/factbook, downloaded 16/06/05

Yerevan State University Republic of Armenia, Beirut: Hamazkayine Educational and Cultural Society

Williamson, H. (2002), *Supporting young people in Europe: principles, policy and practice*, Strasbourg: Council of Europe Publishing

World Bank (2002), *Armenia Poverty Update*, Human Development Sector Unit Report No 24339

World Vision Armenia (2004), Annual Review, Yerevan: World Vision

World Vision Armenia (2005), *Memorandum of Understanding: On the co-operation of the RoA Ministry of Sport and Youth Affairs and Armenia National Office of World Vision International Charitable Organization in the framework of Child Protection Programs*, Yerevan: World Vision

Sales agents for publications of the Council of Europe
Agents de vente des publications du Conseil de l'Europe

BELGIUM/BELGIQUE
La Librairie Europêenne -
The European Bookshop
Rue de l'Orme, 1
BE-1040 BRUXELLES
Tel.: +32 (0)2 231 04 35
Fax: +32 (0)2 735 08 60
E-mail: order@libeurop.be
http://www.libeurop.be

Jean De Lannoy/DL Services
Avenue du Roi 202 Koningslaan
BE-1190 BRUXELLES
Tel.: +32 (0)2 538 43 08
Fax: +32 (0)2 538 08 41
E-mail: jean.de.lannoy@dl-servi.com
http://www.jean-de-lannoy.be

BOSNIA AND HERZEGOVINA/
BOSNIE-HERZÉGOVINE
Robert's Plus d.o.o.
Marka Maruliça 2/V
BA-71000, SARAJEVO
Tel.: + 387 33 640 818
Fax: + 387 33 640 818
E-mail: robertsplus@bih.net.ba

CANADA
Renouf Publishing Co. Ltd.
1-5369 Canotek Road
CA-OTTAWA, Ontario K1J 9J3
Tel.: +1 613 745 2665
Fax: +1 613 745 7660
Toll-Free Tel.: (866) 767-6766
E-mail: order.dept@renoufbooks.com
http://www.renoufbooks.com

CROATIA/CROATIE
Robert's Plus d.o.o.
Marasoviçeva 67
HR-21000, SPLIT
Tel.: + 385 21 315 800, 801, 802, 803
Fax: + 385 21 315 804
E-mail: robertsplus@robertsplus.hr

CZECH REPUBLIC/
RÉPUBLIQUE TCHÈQUE
Suweco CZ, s.r.o.
Klecakova 347
CZ-180 21 PRAHA 9
Tel.: +420 2 424 59 204
Fax: +420 2 848 21 646
E-mail: import@suweco.cz
http://www.suweco.cz

DENMARK/DANEMARK
GAD
Vimmelskaftet 32
DK-1161 KØBENHAVN K
Tel.: +45 77 66 60 00
Fax: +45 77 66 60 01
E-mail: gad@gad.dk
http://www.gad.dk

FINLAND/FINLANDE
Akateeminen Kirjakauppa
PO Box 128
Keskuskatu 1
FI-00100 HELSINKI
Tel.: +358 (0)9 121 4430
Fax: +358 (0)9 121 4242
E-mail: akatilaus@akateeminen.com
http://www.akateeminen.com

FRANCE
La Documentation française
(diffusion/distribution France entière)
124, rue Henri Barbusse
FR-93308 AUBERVILLIERS CEDEX
Tél.: +33 (0)1 40 15 70 00
Fax: +33 (0)1 40 15 68 00
E-mail: commande@ladocumentationfrancaise.fr
http://www.ladocumentationfrancaise.fr

Librairie Kléber
1 rue des Francs Bourgeois
FR-67000 STRASBOURG
Tel.: +33 (0)3 88 15 78 88
Fax: +33 (0)3 88 15 78 80
E-mail: librairie-kleber@coe.int
http://www.librairie-kleber.com

GERMANY/ALLEMAGNE
AUSTRIA/AUTRICHE
UNO Verlag GmbH
August-Bebel-Allee 6
DE-53175 BONN
Tel.: +49 (0)228 94 90 20
Fax: +49 (0)228 94 90 222
E-mail: bestellung@uno-verlag.de
http://www.uno-verlag.de

GREECE/GRÈCE
Librairie Kauffmann s.a.
Stadiou 28
GR-105 64 ATHINAI
Tel.: +30 210 32 55 321
Fax.: +30 210 32 30 320
E-mail: ord@otenet.gr
http://www.kauffmann.gr

HUNGARY/HONGRIE
Euro Info Service
Pannónia u. 58.
PF. 1039
HU-1136 BUDAPEST
Tel.: +36 1 329 2170
Fax: +36 1 349 2053
E-mail: euroinfo@euroinfo.hu
http://www.euroinfo.hu

ITALY/ITALIE
Licosa SpA
Via Duca di Calabria, 1/1
IT-50125 FIRENZE
Tel.: +39 0556 483215
Fax: +39 0556 41257
E-mail: licosa@licosa.com
http://www.licosa.com

MEXICO/MEXIQUE
Mundi-Prensa México, S.A. De C.V.
Río Pánuco, 141 Delegacíon Cuauhtémoc
MX-06500 MÉXICO, D.F.
Tel.: +52 (01)55 55 33 56 58
Fax: +52 (01)55 55 14 67 99
E-mail: mundiprensa@mundiprensa.com.mx
http://www.mundiprensa.com.mx

NETHERLANDS/PAYS-BAS
Roodveldt Import BV
Nieuwe Hemweg 50
NE-1013 CX AMSTERDAM
Tel.: + 31 20 622 8035
Fax.: + 31 20 625 5493
Website: www.publidis.org
Email: orders@publidis.org

NORWAY/NORVÈGE
Akademika
Postboks 84 Blindern
NO-0314 OSLO
Tel.: +47 2 218 8100
Fax: +47 2 218 8103
E-mail: support@akademika.no
http://www.akademika.no

POLAND/POLOGNE
Ars Polona JSC
25 Obroncow Street
PL-03-933 WARSZAWA
Tel.: +48 (0)22 509 86 00
Fax: +48 (0)22 509 86 10
E-mail: arspolona@arspolona.com.pl
http://www.arspolona.com.pl

PORTUGAL
Livraria Portugal
(Dias & Andrade, Lda.)
Rua do Carmo, 70
PT-1200-094 LISBOA
Tel.: +351 21 347 42 82 / 85
Fax: +351 21 347 02 64
E-mail: info@livrariaportugal.pt
http://www.livrariaportugal.pt

RUSSIAN FEDERATION/
FÉDÉRATION DE RUSSIE
Ves Mir
17b, Butlerova ul.
RU-101000 MOSCOW
Tel.: +7 495 739 0971
Fax: +7 495 739 0971
E-mail: orders@vesmirbooks.ru
http://www.vesmirbooks.ru

SPAIN/ESPAGNE
Mundi-Prensa Libros, s.a.
Castelló, 37
ES-28001 MADRID
Tel.: +34 914 36 37 00
Fax: +34 915 75 39 98
E-mail: libreria@mundiprensa.es
http://www.mundiprensa.com

SWITZERLAND/SUISSE
Planetis Sàrl
16 chemin des Pins
CH-1273 ARZIER
Tel.: +41 22 366 51 77
Fax: +41 22 366 51 78
E-mail: info@planetis.ch

UNITED KINGDOM/ROYAUME-UNI
The Stationery Office Ltd
PO Box 29
GB-NORWICH NR3 1GN
Tel.: +44 (0)870 600 5522
Fax: +44 (0)870 600 5533
E-mail: book.enquiries@tso.co.uk
http://www.tsoshop.co.uk

UNITED STATES and CANADA/
ÉTATS-UNIS et CANADA
Manhattan Publishing Co
2036 Albany Post Road
USA-10520 CROTON ON HUDSON, NY
Tel.: +1 914 271 5194
Fax: +1 914 271 5886
E-mail: coe@manhattanpublishing.coe
http://www.manhattanpublishing.com

Council of Europe Publishing/Editions du Conseil de l'Europe
FR-67075 STRASBOURG Cedex
Tel.: +33 (0)3 88 41 25 81 – Fax: +33 (0)3 88 41 39 10 – E-mail: publishing@coe.int – Website: http://book.coe.int